The Dawn of Swatch

The Dawn of Swatch

Timeless Strategies in Business, Marketing, and Entrepreneurship

Omar Merlo and Konstantin Theile

BEP
BUSINESS EXPERT PRESS
Leader in applied, concise business books

The Dawn of Swatch:
Timeless Strategies in Business, Marketing, and Entrepreneurship

Cover design by Charlene Kronstedt

Interior design by S4Carlisle Publishing Services, Chennai, India

First published in 2025 by
Business Expert Press, LLC
222 East 46th Street, New York, NY 10017
www.businessexpertpress.com

ISBN-13: 978-1-63742-872-6 (paperback)
ISBN-13: 978-1-63742-873-3 (e-book)

Marketing Collection

First edition: 2025

10 9 8 7 6 5 4 3 2 1

EU SAFETY REPRESENTATIVE
Mare Nostrum Group B.V.
Mauritskade 21D
1091 GC Amsterdam
The Netherlands
gpsr@mare-nostrum.co.uk

Description

The Dawn of Swatch: Timeless Strategies in Business, Marketing, and Entrepreneurship tells the remarkable story of how a simple plastic watch transformed not just an industry, but the way we think about branding, innovation, and market disruption.

In the early 1980s, the Swiss watch industry was in crisis, losing market share to Japanese quartz watches. Swatch—a bold, affordable, and fashion-forward timepiece—emerged as a game changer, proving that success is not just about technology but about reinventing an industry through marketing, strategy, and visionary leadership.

Through firsthand accounts and analysis, the authors reveal how strategic vision, bold marketing, and unconventional thinking turned Swatch into a global phenomenon. Drawing from insider experiences and business research, they explore the key lessons behind Swatch's early success, offering practical and timeless insights on branding, consumer psychology, differentiation, market-driven innovation, and beyond.

More than just a case study about a successful launch, this book provides actionable lessons for business leaders, entrepreneurs, marketers, and students of strategy. It offers a blueprint for challenging industry norms, crafting compelling brand narratives, and developing market-driving strategies that stand the test of time—insights that are applicable across any industry where innovation, differentiation, and bold decision making drive success.

Contents

List of Figures

Preface

Among many business case studies, the launch of Swatch in the early 1980s stands out as a story of enduring relevance. It illustrates the role of innovation, vision, and strategic risk-taking—qualities that continue to be important in an evolving and competitive business environment. More than just a tale of technology and marketing, Swatch's rise exemplifies the seamless fusion of vision and execution, strategy and intuition. From its disruptive early marketing efforts to its evolution into a global phenomenon, the Swatch story offers valuable lessons in marketing strategy, leadership, innovation, and entrepreneurship, demonstrating how bold decisions and calculated risks can redefine markets, create new opportunities, and inspire both aspiring entrepreneurs and seasoned executives alike.

The success of the Swatch launch and the revival of the Swiss watch industry in the 1980s were the result of a unique combination of factors. Operational restructuring, centralized manufacturing, leveraging economies of scale, and a strong cultural narrative of "Swiss-made" quality, all played critical roles in the industry's turnaround. The focus of this book is intentionally on the marketing, strategic, and entrepreneurial dimensions of Swatch's success. While not exhaustive in addressing every determinant of Swatch's impact, this approach allows us to derive practical lessons specifically tailored for managers and entrepreneurs.

What sets this book apart is its insider perspective, offering readers a glimpse behind the curtains of Swatch's birth to its global success. I had the privilege of working on this book with Dr. Konstantin Theile (the first Marketing Director of Swatch, and a wonderful coauthor and friend), who was a key member of the early Swatch team and played a significant role in influencing the success of the brand. Konstantin witnessed the story unfold firsthand, navigated its highs and lows, and learned and shared invaluable lessons along the way.

This book is not just about Swatch or watches; it draws broader implications for today's business practitioners. We examine enduring managerial principles, explore parallels with current companies and leaders, and connect Swatch's lessons to today's fast-paced industries. By analyzing how modern companies navigate similar challenges, we demonstrate that the Swatch story is full of practical lessons for any business leader. Its insights extend far beyond the watch industry, offering valuable strategies and inspiration to professionals across diverse sectors.

Ultimately, Swatch's early days are a testament to resilience, creativity, and leadership, reminding us that while markets and trends may shift, certain principles of success remain constant. As you journey through this narrative, I hope you will find inspiration and enduring insights that are as relevant to today's business environment as they were when Swatch first revolutionized the watch industry.

Many people contributed to the making of this book, and I'm especially grateful to Barbara Duffek, Neil Ghosh, Jaka Levstek, and Tanita Yonel for their input throughout the process. Their contributions enriched both the content and the process of bringing this book to life.

—Dr. Omar Merlo, Imperial Business School, London, UK

***

By a fortunate stroke of luck, I found myself in the right place at the right time when Dr. Ernst Thomke, the visionary CEO of ETA SA and the mastermind behind the Swatch project, was searching for someone to develop the international marketing strategy for Swatch and manage its global sales.

Thomke, a truly exceptional transformational leader, inspired the entire Swatch team to view the extraordinary as not just possible but achievable and actionable. He championed creativity, innovation, and a bold willingness to take risks. His remarkable ability to identify the potential in unconventional ideas and nurture them through open dialogue was instrumental to the project's success.

Reflecting on this experience, I realize that these lessons have profoundly shaped my professional journey.

I also learned that (almost) anything is possible when you lead a team that is both excellent and open-minded, one that embraces innovation while empowering its members with trust, responsibility, and freedom.

Success, as I've come to understand, is rarely the product of a single individual—it is the collective achievement of a dedicated team.

While chance and serendipity play their roles, they must be recognized, assessed, and acted upon to transform the extraordinary into a tangible success. The famous quote by Thomas A. Edison, "Genius is 1 percent inspiration and 99 percent perspiration," aptly applies to the Swatch project. We were fortunate to have many people, both within and outside the company, contribute unusual and innovative ideas, which we eagerly embraced and brought to life through a great deal of "perspiration."

The inspiration for this book came from Dr. Omar Merlo, who has long been a close friend and frequently invites me as a guest lecturer. I am deeply grateful to him for encouraging and helping to bring this idea to fruition.

—Dr. Konstantin Theile, Küsnacht, Switzerland

CHAPTER 1

Meine Damen und Herren

Zurich, Tuesday, March 1, 1983. The sun was shining in Switzerland, across the city's skyline, the atmosphere charged with anticipation. A place famous for chiseled architecture sweeping across a picturesque and pristine landscape was today unveiling a new watch brand.

The previous weeks had been a whirlwind of activity in the industry, whispers of a revolutionary new idea in the air. Zurich, a city that had always been a hub of innovation, was buzzing with the spirit of creativity and enterprise. The sun's rays made Zurich's famous lake glitter like a polished timepiece, offering a beautiful metaphorical and macrocosmic mirror of the events about to unfold.

The anticipation was palpable, the sense of corresponding excitement reflected in the eyes of the journalists and reporters who had been invited to attend the impending press conference.

The imposing figure of Ernst Thomke presided over the expansive glass table, his authoritative presence filling the room. Aged 43, he commanded the respect of everyone in the company as the CEO of ETA S.A. His crisp gray suit, perfectly tailored to his frame, exuded a sense of power and control. Above his lip, a robust chestnut moustache added to his impressive demeanor.

To his right sat Anton Bally, the Head of Production at ETA. Despite only being in his late 30s, he was already a legend in the world of watchmaking. His pioneering work in quartz movement design had earned him the reputation of being a master craftsman. As the descendant of a long line of watchmakers, he carried the weight of his family's legacy on his broad shoulders.

Seated to Thomke's left was Konstantin Theile, the latest addition to the ETA team. A youthful 32-year-old, he had joined in September 1982 with the somewhat unwieldy title of "Marketing Manager for South America and the Middle East (including India and Africa)." In this role, he was responsible for overseeing the marketing and sales of watch movements in those regions.

However, just after 3 months on the job, Theile had grown restless. In December 1982, he confided in Thomke that he was ready for a new challenge. Impressed by his ambition, Thomke offered him the job of Head of Marketing and Sales for a mysterious top-secret watch project that had been in the works for 3 years. Theile's eyes lit up with excitement as he listened to Thomke's proposal. His interest was immediately piqued. He eagerly accepted the challenge, perceiving that this was the opportunity of a lifetime. Theile couldn't wait to sink his teeth into this new ETA project.

ETA was a Swiss company nestled in the scenic town of Grenchen, steeped in a rich and illustrious history of watch movement manufacturing. Its lineage could be traced all the way back to 1793, a testament to its enduring legacy and unparalleled expertise in watchmaking. Thomke had been at the helm of ETA since 1978. His visionary leadership had overseen numerous groundbreaking projects, each one pushing the boundaries of innovation.

One example of this originality was Anton Bally's Delirium watch, a true marvel in the world of timepieces. Measuring a mere 1.98 mm in thickness, it was hailed as the thinnest watch ever designed. Despite its astronomical price tag of CHF 5,000, the Delirium bore witness to ETA's boundless ingenuity and technical prowess. While not a commercial success, it remains to this day a pioneering gem in the watchmaking world.

On Tuesday, March 1, 1983, the large audience was effervescing with energy in the minutes before Thomke's speech. With a confident stride and a twinkle in his eye, he finally stood up then began his address:

"Meine Damen und Herren!"

Thomke spoke of ETA S.A.'s latest project, a game-changing watch that would revolutionize the industry. He described in detail the technology behind it, the story of its development, and the planned marketing strategy (Figure 1.1).

The journalists and reporters in the room scrambled to capture every word from his lips, their pens furiously scribbling in their notepads. Thomke's announcement was nothing short of groundbreaking: ETA S.A. was about to unleash a revolutionary timepiece onto the market.

Figure 1.1 The Swatch launch press conference in 1983, featuring Anton Bally (left), Ernst Thomke (center) and Konstantin Theile (right)

Source: Photo courtesy of SRF/Tagesschau (March 1, 1983)

A watch that was both high quality and affordable, crafted entirely in Switzerland, and made...wait for it...from plastic!

Its name? Swatch.

As the audience hung onto his every word, Thomke could not hide his passion and enthusiasm for the project. His gestures and expressions spoke for themselves, conveying unwavering belief and determination in the product and its potential for completely disrupting the market. As his words tumbled out, Thomke's conviction in Swatch's potential only grew stronger. Beside him, Bally and Theile could not help but nod in approval, captivated as they were by his words. As Thomke's powerful speech reached its conclusion, the room erupted into a deafening round of applause.

Numerous questions from the press followed, which the Swatch staff, seated behind the table, responded to skillfully and with similar enthusiasm, building a feverish energy for the product that was to come.

For members of the press corps still remaining unconvinced, the inclusion of a freshly minted Swatch Jelly Original in their media package quickly dispelled any doubts. This unique avant-garde timepiece, featuring a transparent plastic case and band, was a true marvel, unlike any watch they had ever seen.

The future of the Swiss watch industry was on the brink of transformation, Thomke and his dedicated team at ETA the frontrunners. The press, and most of Switzerland, were elated about the arrival of the Swatch. They couldn't stop talking about it and were counting down to its release. The buzz surrounding this new plastic watch was contagious—everyone wanted to get their hands on one.

Yet while the public was swept up in fervor, the response from industry insiders had been anything but positive. From the very beginning, the team behind the Swatch had to deal with constant ridicule and criticism. Watch experts scoffed at the idea of a plastic watch, dismissing it as a cheap and disposable product. They couldn't understand how a watch with only 51 parts, screwed and welded together by machines, could ever be successful.

Even within ETA, most people who were not involved in the project were puzzled. To them, the Swatch went against everything the Swiss watch industry stood for. It was too mass-produced, too brightly colored—anathema to the meticulously crafted watches they were used to. They even felt the flavor of betrayal.

When the Swatch had been test-marketed a few months before the 1983 launch in the United States, the response had been lackluster at best. Retailers had shown no enthusiasm for the product; instead, it was met with skepticism from most watch experts. In fact, the Swatch project was a bona fide joke within the industry.

Thomke's motley crew of watchmaking rebels stood firm. They refused to let the naysayers bring them down. They were confident something special had been produced, something that would revolutionize the watch industry. And frankly, they were desperate for it to succeed. They had no Plan B. ETA, and most other Swiss watch companies, had been flirting with financial disaster for years, the end seemed nigh.

Reinforced by such resolute focus, Thomke and the Swatch team's dreams were fulfilled. Following the press conference in Zurich, not only was the Swatch hailed as "positive news from the watch industry for once" and a "revolution in watchmaking technology," masses of people also flocked in their droves to buy them.

Swatch became a breath of fresh air in an industry that had become stagnant and predictable. It was vibrant, fun, and accessible to everyone, breaking the traditional mold of Swiss watches. With its plastic casing and integrated movement, what might have seemed vulgar and disposable to some, it represented a new era of watchmaking to so many others. Despite the initial doubts and criticism of watch experts, the Swatch proved to be a huge success, selling over a million pieces in just a few months. Stocks ran out before the inventory could be replenished. Before long, Swiss media outlets were referring to it as an "unparalleled phenomenon and a bona fide craze."

Masses of customers flooded the once-struggling Swiss watch industry with a steady stream of funds, allowing them to experience the advantages of large-scale production and economies of scale. For the first time, the low-priced Japanese quartz competitors were kept at bay. The Swatch had shown that sometimes going against the grain and taking risks can lead to great success; it was an example of the power of innovation and determination overcoming even the harshest of criticism. In 1984, *Fortune* magazine in the United States recognized the Swatch as one of the top 12 "Products of the Year," alongside the American Express Platinum Card and Apple Macintosh.

The Swatch brand would eventually go on to transform into Swatch Group, the biggest watchmaking conglomerate in the world. This diversified global holding company now possesses a vast range of brands, spanning all price levels.

But where did the Swatch brand name originally come from? The most popular account (and the one the Swatch Group itself seems to endorse these days) is that it was derived from the phrase "Second + Watch." This is based on the idea that Swatch was not just a watch, but a fashion accessory that could be mixed and matched to suit one's outfit and mood. The Swatch was meant to be collected and cherished, not just as a simple timekeeping device, but also as one that people could have several of. And then, as the story goes, later on it became "Swiss + Watch."

However, the real story might be slightly different. The name more likely came from "Sport + Watch," as in the very early days, the initial positioning of the Swatch was aimed at the sports market. This shorthand was likely the brainchild of marketing consultant Franz Sprecher, who had provided the very first marketing input into the project leading up to the launch.

Sprecher believed that the watch's sporty and active design would appeal to a profitable market, namely, sports enthusiasts—and appeal it did. Sportspeople were drawn to the Swatch's durability and waterproof capabilities, a feature that set it apart from all the other cheap watches on the market.

Swatch was a timepiece that could be used for any manner of sporting activity, with its waterproof nature, meaning it could be used for swimming. People would wear their Swatch in the shower. All the while Swatch's timekeeping was perfect. This technical advantage was a game changer, and Swatch quickly gained a competitive edge in the lower end of the market as a sporty watch.

Then, as the brand grew and expanded globally, the narrative shifted. In 1983, a U.S. TV commercial changed the marketing landscape. The advertising agency McCann Erickson saw the potential in combining the words "Swiss" and "Watch" to create a compelling narrative around the iconic name we know today. Swatch became known as "Swiss + Watch"—a symbol of quality, precision, and luxury. Given Thomke and his team's global ambitions, this narrative was a perfect fit for the brand.

In 1983, ETA's Swiss competitors were not just quick—they were lightning fast, sprinting to keep pace with the revolutionary Swatch. The watch had ignited the spark of creativity in its rivals, with Mondaine launching the edgy M-Watch and Fortis introducing the ID-Watch. It was a race to the top, as shoppers at Swiss retailers like Migros and Inter Discount were presented with alluring alternatives to the Swatch.

Christmas of 1983 saw Swiss children eagerly unwrapping gifts, their hearts racing with anticipation as they laid their eyes on a Swatch-shaped box under the tree. Alas, for many of them excitement was soon replaced with bitter disappointment, as they tore open the wrapping to reveal a mere imitation, bearing a name that sounded oh-so-similar, but wasn't quite right.

In fairness, it wasn't just the lower price that had attracted parents to those Swatch clones. The entire Swatch phenomenon had exceeded all sales expectations, and in Switzerland all Swatch watches had sold out within weeks of the launch, leaving consumers with no choice but to seek out alternatives that simply did not measure up.

The frustration and dismay that swept through the land as the one and only Swatch remained out of reach were palpable. As for those poor children—well, let's just say their Christmases were not so merry after all! This also offers a sobering reminder that while products, features, and designs can be easily replicated, brands possess a unique power to evoke intense emotions that cannot be easily duplicated.

CHAPTER 2

A Brief History of the Watch Industry

The Swiss watch industry was on the brink of collapse in the early 1980s, as competition from cheaper and more durable watches flooded in from the United States and Japan. The future looked bleak, with many predicting the downfall of traditional Swiss watchmakers.

The industry's crisis during the 1970s and early 1980s extended far beyond the rise of quartz technology. Economic downturns, including the oil crisis, reduced consumer spending and heightened the appeal of less expensive alternatives. Additionally, Swiss watchmakers struggled to adapt to global market shifts. Their reliance on fragmented production systems, compounded by strong labor unions and resistance to change, left them unable to compete with the streamlined and cost-efficient manufacturing processes employed by Japanese brands like Seiko and Citizen.

The inability to profitably scale quartz production only deepened the financial disarray for Swiss companies. Swiss watchmakers initially viewed quartz technology as a threat to their mechanical expertise, and its latent potential to redefine the meaning of a watch went unnoticed. This oversight allowed competitors to seize market share, positioning quartz as an affordable and practical alternative. It wasn't until Swatch reimagined quartz not just as a technological innovation but also as a vehicle for cultural and emotional resonance that its transformative power was fully realized.

While collaborative efforts by the Swiss government, banks, and industry stakeholders provided temporary relief during the sector's most vulnerable periods, these corporatist structures also fostered inefficiencies. By prioritizing short-term stability and protecting established players, corporatism sometimes hindered the industry's ability to embrace disruptive changes.

By 1980, Japan's watch industry had surpassed Switzerland in global market share, a stark reversal of dominance from just two decades earlier. Then, a glimmer of hope emerged in the form of the Swatch. But before we unravel the brilliance of Swatch's strategy and global success, let us first delve into the world of the watch industry—a world where precision and craftsmanship reign supreme, where every detail quite literally counts, and every watch tells a story.

Despite the industry's crisis, the Swiss watchmaking tradition remained rooted in centuries of craftsmanship and innovation. The art of timekeeping, shaped by pioneers like Peter Henlein, reflects a legacy of meticulous precision and creativity that has captivated the world since its inception. At the dawn of the sixteenth century, Peter Henlein, a skilled German clockmaker, created the first modern pocket watch, earning him the title of the father of modern timekeeping and, arguably, the entire watchmaking industry.

These early clock watches gained popularity in the 1500s and were commonly attached to clothing or worn as a necklace. However, with only an hour hand, they were not accurate timekeepers and served more as a symbol of wealth for the affluent. In the year 1577, the invention of the minute hand was finally credited to the Swiss clockmaker Jost Bürgi.

As the industry evolved, innovation flourished. In 1657, the "balance spring" was invented (with dispute over whether it was Christiaan Huygens or Robert Hooke who made the groundbreaking discovery). Essentially, a "balance spring" is a delicate and tightly wound coil that regulates the movements, or vibrations, of the balance within a timepiece responsible for the ticking of a watch.

This innovation significantly enhanced the accuracy and exactness of watches. When King Charles II of England introduced the waistcoat in 1675, it led to the transformation of watches into pocket style to fit in the waistcoat's pockets. And during the beginning of the 1700s, timepieces began utilizing rubies as pivots to decrease friction at vital junctures and enhance the precision and longevity of watches.

Watchmaking became an esteemed profession, with master artisans establishing respected ateliers across Switzerland, each contributing to the country's rising hegemony in the realm of timekeeping. From Geneva to

La Chaux-de-Fonds, these skilled artisans honed their craft, their names becoming legendary in the annals of horological history.

Swiss watchmaker Abraham Louis Perrelet, one of the pioneers of precision watchmaking, is often credited for inventing a self-winding mechanism for watches around the year 1780. Then it is believed that the first actual wristwatch was created in 1810 by Abraham-Louis Breguet for the Queen of Naples. He was a renowned timepiece designer from Neuchâtel, known for his visionary skills and revolutionary contributions to the field.

Breguet's Paris atelier became a pilgrimage site for those seeking precision timekeeping. His watches were coveted for their intricate designs and innovative complications. The creations were not just functional but were also works of art, satisfying the aesthetic desires and sensibilities of his clientele.

Breguet's genius extended beyond aesthetics. As he pioneered the balance between precision and portability, the way was paved for the wristwatch. This revolutionary concept would change the course of timekeeping, with Breguet's masterpiece for the Queen of Naples marking the beginning of a new era. The wristwatch evolved from a fashion accessory to a necessary tool, offering both convenience and accuracy.

Women's watches initially gained popularity in the late nineteenth century. Affluent ladies began incorporating small, stylish watches into their bracelets. This served as both a practical solution to carrying large pocket watches and a fashion statement. These watches were not known for their accuracy but, rather, for their aesthetic appeal. They were also more of a passing trend rather than serious timekeeping instruments, as men who typically carried pocket watches dismissed them and claimed they would "rather don a skirt than wear a wristwatch."

Men eventually also began considering wristwatches for both functional and fashionable purposes in the early twentieth century, leading the wristwatch to become a widespread phenomenon. During this time, women were sporting "wristlets," the forerunner to the modern wristwatch. These early wristlets, such as the Rolex "Princess" and Cartier "Tonneau" models, were not only aesthetically pleasing but also marked a major shift in the timekeeping industry.

The wristwatch was no longer just a fashion accessory but a necessary tool that offered both convenience and accuracy. In 1904, aviation pioneer Alberto Santos-Dumont collaborated with his friend Louis Cartier to create a watch that would allow him to accurately track his flight performance while keeping both hands on the controls. Cartier enlisted the help of master watchmaker Edmond Jaeger to produce a prototype for what would become the first-ever pilot watch, the Cartier Santos-Dumont.

Meanwhile, in 1905, visionary Hans Wilsdorf established Wilsdorf and Davis in London and, 3 years later, opened an office in Switzerland, laying the foundation for the renowned Swiss luxury watch company, Rolex.

During World War I, the importance of synchronized timekeeping was highlighted, as delays could have serious consequences. As a result, soldiers were equipped with "trench watches," which housed pocket watch movements within large and bulky wristwatches, with the crown positioned at 12 o'clock, resembling a pocket watch.

In the mid- twentieth century, a significant revolution shook the watch industry. Before the 1950s, timepieces were crafted by expert jewelry makers and micro-technicians, who meticulously assembled over 100 intricate parts. They were adorned with precious gems like rubies and sapphires, not only adding a touch of opulence but also increasing their durability against mechanical wear.

These watches were considered a valuable investment, sold by esteemed jewelers and high-end department stores, often passed down as cherished family heirlooms. Most watchmakers earned their profits from repairing these exquisite timepieces.

However, in 1951, a game-changing company in United States shattered this traditional approach by introducing disposable watches under the brand name, Timex. Suddenly, watches were no longer regarded as treasured jewelry pieces but, rather, as functional tools with a limited lifespan, designed solely to tell time until they inevitably stopped doing so.

The technology behind the Timex was a result of the company's tireless efforts during World War II, where they developed a revolutionary method of using hard alloy metals instead of jewels in their mechanical movements. Not only did this drastically reduce production costs, but it also opened the pathway for automated production, making Timex watches even more affordable.

Designed with simplicity in mind, they boasted a strictly functional appearance with cheap exterior materials. And with no way to open them up for repairs, they were marketed as disposable watches. Despite their humble origins, Timex watches quickly rose to the top of the market, capturing the hearts of one out of every three watch buyers in the United States by the end of the 1950s.

Timex's iconic tagline, "It takes a lickin' and keeps on tickin'," spoke volumes about the unbreakable spirit of their watches. In fact, the company's extensive television advertising campaign featuring outrageous "torture tests"—like subjecting a Timex to a week-long spin in a vacuum cleaner or taping one to a giant lobster's claw—only further reinforced the message of strength and reliability. So as the world's demand for watches continued to grow, Timex emerged as a dominant player, surpassing all other manufacturers in terms of units sold by 1970.

Meanwhile, during Timex's rise to dominance in the watch industry, several Japanese companies were making their mark in the market. Companies such as Hattori-Seiko and Citizen were commanding the Japanese market and expanding their presence to other regions like Asia, Europe, and North America.

In a groundbreaking move in 1969, Seiko introduced the world's first quartz watch, posing a threat to traditional mechanical watches. The Seiko Quartz Astron revolutionized technology, boasting an unparalleled accuracy of just $\pm$ 5 seconds per month, far surpassing that of any mechanical movement. Its compact motor conserved energy by moving the second hand only once per second, a revolutionary feature for wristwatches. The battery also boasted an impressive lifespan of a full year.

By 1970, the once-dominant Swiss watchmaking industry saw its global market share plummet to a mere 42 percent, from a staggering 80 percent in 1946. This sudden decline caused a ripple effect throughout the industry, leaving traditional watchmakers scrambling to keep pace. The introduction and mass production of quartz technology by the Japanese recalibrated the playing field altogether.

Quartz technology watches utilized integrated circuits, making them not only more precise than their mechanical counterparts but also more versatile and cost-effective to produce. This posed a major challenge for traditional watchmakers, as the competition became fierce. However, it wasn't just about the technology—these watches were not only functional but were also aesthetically pleasing. With luxurious gold and silver plating, they imitated the traditional appearance of expensive Swiss-made mechanical watches. This seamless blend of form and function caught the world's attention.

While quartz watches would eventually gain a reputation as affordable timepieces for the masses, the 1969 Astron, for instance, boasted a distinctly lavish 18k gold case, putting it in direct competition with high-end Swiss watches. Eventually, as cheaper quartz watches flooded the market, the competition shifted to the lower end of the spectrum.

And for the Swiss, the Quartz Revolution merely made a bad situation even worse. The country's watch industry's decline in the 1970s had already commenced prior to the Quartz Revolution, due to various factors. The economic conditions during this time, such as the oil crisis and recession, led to uncertainty and reduced consumer spending.

The expensive nature of Swiss mechanical watches made them less desirable in the face of economic instability. Additionally, Swiss watchmakers were hesitant to adopt new technologies, disregarding quartz as a passing trend by way of example.

However, by the time they did recognize the significance of quartz, Japanese companies had already established dominance in the market. The Swiss struggled to catch up and faced challenges in revamping their production processes. They attempted to maintain their competitive edge by producing more affordable watches. However, this came at the expense of sacrificing their reputation for quality and tradition. Inefficiency and high production costs were also major hindrances for the Swiss.

While the Japanese implemented an efficient and streamlined production process, allowing them to create high-quality watches at a lower cost through standardized methods and global distribution, the Swiss really started lagging behind. They also had to contend with highly unionized and costly labor, as well as complacent and inadequate management that resisted change.

While the Swiss offered a wide variety of watch models, the Japanese focused on perfecting and adapting a much smaller number. Furthermore, currency issues posed a challenge for the Swiss, as the Japanese had the advantage of a stable currency, making their watches more affordable compared to the Swiss whose franc reached record levels. This resulted in Swiss watches being perceived as more expensive and less valuable to customers.

By 1979, Hattori-Seiko had become the world's largest watch company, producing a staggering 22 million watches annually. And while Timex still held the top spot in the under-$50 category, it had lost significant ground to Seiko in the above-$50 category. The battle for dominance was intense, but the Japanese manufacturers seemed to have the upper hand.

Yet it wasn't just about the numbers. These watches evoked strong emotions in people. They were more than just timekeeping devices; they were symbols of style, sophistication, and status. And as the world fell in love with quartz watches, the Japanese manufacturers continued to innovate and dominate the market.

By 1984, more than three-quarters of the watches sold around the world were based on quartz technology, and Japan's Citizen had overtaken everyone to become the overall global leader in both movement and finished watch production volumes. The number of Swiss watch exports declined significantly from 84 million to 31 million units annually between the years 1975 and 1984. This decline also had a negative impact on employment within the industry, with the number of workers decreasing from 90,000 to 45,000.

Swiss watches, once the country's crown jewels, faced an uncertain future as the world grew captivated by the allure of sleek, inexpensive time-pieces originating from the Far East. Through the 1970s and into the early 1980s, the Swiss saw their market share shrink and their once-flourishing industry falter. For the first time in their illustrious history, the future of Swiss watchmaking appeared deeply uncertain. Amid this backdrop of turmoil and transformation, a remarkable convergence of global trends was beginning to reshape industries and open new opportunities for com-panies willing to adapt.

The 1980s marked a period of significant global economic change. Rising disposable incomes in many developed nations, coupled with the expansion of consumer markets, created a growing demand for products that combined affordability with aspirational appeal. Consumers increasingly sought value for money while becoming more attuned to brands that reflected their lifestyles and aspirations. This shift opened the door for businesses to deliver innovative products that could bridge quality and accessibility.

Equally pivotal was the transformation of consumer behavior. The 1980s witnessed a surge in fashion's role as a form of self-expression, with accessories becoming key tools for crafting individual identity. Products that could reflect personal style and adapt to evolving trends found themselves at the center of consumer demand. Companies that understood and catered to this desire for personalization and variety were well-positioned to thrive.

At the same time, globalization was accelerating, exposing consumers to a broader range of products from around the world. This shift offered both challenges and opportunities, as brands needed to navigate increasingly diverse markets while leveraging the expanding reach of international trade and media. Companies that developed bold, culturally resonant strategies to appeal across borders could gain significant competitive advantages.

These global economic shifts, coupled with evolving consumer preferences, offered fertile ground for companies that could effectively harness these trends. Aligning with the growing demand for affordability, personalization, and accessibility presented a significant opportunity, but success was far from guaranteed. Businesses willing to take bold risks and innovate had the potential to transform industries and challenge the boundaries of traditional markets, yet the path to achieving such outcomes was uncertain and fraught with challenges.

CHAPTER 3

The Swatch Concept

The Swiss watchmakers of the late 1970s and early 1980s were facing a significant crisis, encountering difficulties with the acquisition of new technologies and integration of them into their production system. And they were up against a new, cutting-edge technology: quartz watches. They found themselves with no idea how to compete. Some watchmakers were even reluctant to try, believing that electronic watches were unreliable and beneath their high standards. Yet while they clung to their traditional ways, the rest of the world was embracing the convenience and precision of quartz. In the eyes of the Swiss, quartz watches were nothing more than a passing fad, a mere trinket to be discarded.

Ironically, the first quartz watch originated in the Swiss city of Neuchâtel in 1967. The Swiss, renowned for their meticulous craftsmanship and traditional watchmaking, had unwittingly given birth to a technological nightmare, which later proved a site of bitterness. Like a modern-day Frankenstein's monster, the quartz watch was met with disgust and horror by its very creators. The once proud Swiss watchmakers tried to bury their creation, hoping to distance themselves from the cold, lifeless ticking of the quartz movement.

Then as the world embraced the precision and convenience of the quartz watch, the Swiss were forced to confront their own fears and insecurities. The very technology they had shunned and rejected was now dominating the watch industry and threatening to render their traditional watches obsolete. It presented a cruel twist of fate, a telling reminder of how quickly progress can sweep away old and cherished ways.

The Swiss watchmakers, once revered and respected, were now being seen as old-fashioned and even anachronistic. These once master craftsmen struggled to adapt to the changing times; they became more and more like the characters in a tragic play, emotions running high as they clung to their traditional values and beliefs. The once familiar world of watchmaking had become a complex and intriguing battleground, with the Swiss fighting to maintain identity and relevance in the marketplace.

The stubbornness and reluctance of industry leaders to adapt would lead to their downfall. The two largest Swiss companies, ASUAG and SSIH, were hemorrhaging money, unable to keep up with the Japanese giants like Seiko and Casio. ASUAG, with its ownership of over 100 brands, including Longines and Rado, was drowning in losses. SSIH, a private company controlling brands like Omega and Tissot, experienced the same fate.

The crisis did not stop there. The Swiss also faced challenges with the production of quartz, as they needed to produce a certain quantity to break even and turn a profit. To make matters worse, a joint venture between ASUAG and Phillips, created to produce the necessary quartz for watch movements, was a massive failure. As a result, Phillips eventually pulled out of the joint venture, leaving the Swiss in a state of desperation.

With losses mounting, the top management at ASUAG were forced to confront the harsh reality of something major needing to change. They had to find a way to make quartz watchmaking profitable to compete with the Japanese, but could they overcome their pride to adapt to the changing times?

By the end of the 1970s, it became painfully clear just how bad the situation had become. Headlines screamed of mass layoffs, reduced working hours, and shuttered factories. The once booming industry was now a shadow of its former self, with the number of employees plummeting to only 30,000.

As protests erupted, the Swiss watch industry was nearly laid to rest, symbolic of a bygone era. Foreign newspapers, sensing the imminent collapse, declared it was teetering on the "brink of ruin" or had "already met its demise." The future was bleak, and all hope was lost. The once proud and prosperous industry confronted its darkest hour, no visible light at the end of the tunnel.

A group of Swiss banks found themselves facing a dire situation. They had made risky loans to the struggling watch companies. Their entire fortune was on the line. Desperate for a solution, in 1982 they turned to Nicolas Hayek, the founder of Hayek Engineering, a management consulting firm based in Zurich.

Hayek had an extensive track record of helping restructure businesses, making him well-equipped to take on this new challenge. Born in Beirut, he had studied mathematics and physics in France before moving to Switzerland with his wife, Marianne. But it wasn't until he temporarily took over his father-in-law's engineering firm in Bern that he gained an understanding of the challenges of industrial manufacturing.

When he heard about the banks' plan to liquidate the watch companies, he was incensed, thereafter presenting a plan to restructure the industry. Hayek identified issues in products, policies, distribution, and leadership. But his most audacious and controversial recommendation was proposing the merger of the two companies ASUAG and SSIH. Despite initial hesitation, at the beginning of 1983, the banks agreed to Hayek's plan. They put him in charge of overseeing this alliance. With an injection of 1 billion Swiss francs, Hayek set to work restructuring the companies.

Fortuitously, during this period of restructuring and infusion of funds, a team of exceptional engineers within one of ASUAG's subsidiaries had already been quietly laying the groundwork for the eventual creation of the Swatch. Despite commonly being linked to the birth of the Swatch, Hayek's participation did not commence until later.

In 1986 Hayek became investor and CEO of SMH (Société de Microélectronique et d'Horlogérie), which was renamed Swatch Group in 1988. By the time he had joined, all the key elements—the technological advancements, automation, the vertical integration strategy, the positioning as a fashion accessory telling time, and the marketing concept—had already been developed (between 1978 and 1982). However, Hayek would go on to become a strong and decisive promoter of the Swatch. He contributed significantly to its success in the years following the 1983 market launch in Switzerland, France, Germany, the UK, and the United States.

While ASUAG and SSIH were being restructured during those turbulent years, their management had been toying with an audacious idea—a watch that was affordable yet stylish. This concept was not entirely new, drawing inspiration from the Roskopf watch and its visionary creator, George Roskopf.

Roskopf, a German-Swiss watchmaker who resided and worked in La Chaux-de-Fonds from 1829 to 1889, was fuelled by idealism and a desire to provide affordable, high-quality timepieces for the laboring class. In 1860, he embarked on a mission to design a watch that could be sold for only 20 Swiss francs, without compromising on quality, simplicity, or durability.

This watch was aptly named *montre proletaire*—the laborer's watch. The Roskopf watch was a revolutionary breakthrough in the Swiss watchmaking industry, being the first to enter the realm of mass marketing and cheap production. In 1867, Roskopf successfully produced 2,000 watches, marking the beginning of his business venture. In just 3 years, his orders had increased 10-fold, with 20,000 watches being produced.

The success of the Roskopf watch caught the attention of ASUAG's top management, who were facing the daunting challenge of the quartz crisis. They saw an opportunity in it: a watch that could be mass-produced in large quantities at low cost. But this was no easy feat. They had to think outside the box and come up with a strategy that would set them apart from their competitors, needing to create a watch that would appeal to the masses, not only affordable but also high quality.

Enter the determined and ambitious Ernst Thomke. Born in the bilingual city of Bienne, nestled on the border of the Franco-German language regions of Switzerland, Thomke's journey began with an apprenticeship in mechanics at the movement manufacturer ETA SA. But his insatiable thirst for knowledge led him to pursue studies in natural sciences and medicine while working full-time. With a relentless pursuit of knowledge and development, he became a doctor in 1975 before setting his sights on higher education in management and marketing at INSEAD in France. After a successful stint in research at the renowned Beecham pharmaceutical group in Switzerland and Sweden, he returned to ETA SA in 1978, taking the reins of the ASUAG subsidiary as CEO.

Thomke had a grand, audacious vision at ETA. He was determined to reclaim market share in the low-price watch segment, yearning for nothing less than the crown jewel: the "cheapest and best watch of all time." And not just any watch, but one that was 100 percent made in Switzerland, a pinnacle of quality and precision.

Driven by this ambition, Thomke launched an internal competition for his team of engineers, challenging them to create the seemingly impossible. But as the days turned into weeks, the weeks into months, nothing suitable materialized. Thomke's frustration grew. He had high expectations of his team, but they seemed to be falling short. As the competition dragged on for over a year, Thomke faced mounting challenges that threatened to dim his once-bright vision.

One morning in early 1980, tension filled the office. Thomke walked in, his usual calm demeanor replaced by visible frustration. He slammed his briefcase down on the desk, glaring at an invoice: He could not believe what he was looking at. CHF 500,000 for an injection molding machine? The astronomical price tag made his blood boil. As he paced back and forth, his mind raced with questions. Who had ordered this machine? And why on earth did they need it? His assistant hurried around, urgently trying to identify the source of the problem, but Thomke was visibly frustrated. He spoke sharply into the phone, his tone firm and unwavering. Someone had to take responsibility, and he was prepared to take decisive action.

Just when the situation seemed unbearable, the door opened. In walked a reserved figure, Elmar Mock, a young engineer with a passion for plastics. As he stood before Thomke, his eyes downcast and shoulders tense, he likely feared the worst. After all, in the past year alone, 4,000 employees had been let go; he could easily be next. But as Thomke voiced his frustration, something in Mock shifted. He straightened his posture, his eyes reflecting a newfound resolve—and perhaps even a touch of defiance.

Mock had always been something of a mystery in the office. While his intellect and fascination with polymers were well known, he had a particular interest that set him apart: a strong desire to work with an injection molding machine. These machines functioned similarly to an industrial version of a Play-Doh factory, except instead of soft dough, they used plastic pellets, heating and softening them before injecting them into a mold. Once the mold was filled, the machine cooled the plastic, solidifying it into a finished, ready-to-use object.

In essence, Mock had placed an order for a giant Play-Doh factory without any authority or approval, knowingly risking his job to make his dream a reality. As Thomke voiced his frustration, Mock reached into a folder and pulled out a colorful sketch. The vibrant display boasted a playful combination of pink and blue tones, exuding a childlike charm. It was the sketch of a watch made from plastic—a seemingly simple concept but one holding significant originality and potential. Mock explained his vision to Thomke, his voice growing more confident and passionate with each word.

He explained that the sketch was the unexpected result of a fruitful trip to Germany. A few weeks earlier, Mock had attended a training session at the University of Esslingen with his ETA colleague Jacques Müller, a highly accomplished watch engineer with a sharp mind and a curious spirit (Figure 3.1).

From a young age, Müller had been fascinated by horology, dedicating himself to studying and mastering the art of watchmaking. His passion and expertise were unmatched. By 1980, he had already designed several watch movements from scratch, each one a masterpiece of precision and innovation. From the humblest of cheap movements to the most exquisite and high-end ones, Müller poured his heart and soul into every piece he created.

Yet it was more than just his technical skills that made Müller stand out. He was a man of unshakable confidence, a true visionary who never backed down from a challenge. When presented with the seemingly impossible task of creating a high-quality watch that could be produced for just a few francs and proudly bear the label "100% Swiss made," Müller

Figure 3.1 A 1983 Swiss TV appearance by Elmar Mock (left) and Jacques Müller (right)

Source: Photo courtesy of SRF/Karussell (April 7, 1983).

didn't flinch. Instead, he saw it as an opportunity to push himself even further, to reach new heights and thereby prove his talent.

On that day in Esslingen, Mock and Müller decided to sneak away from the training course, finding themselves in a cozy local pub. Sipping on frothy pints of beer, their minds buzzed with ideas about how to win Thomke's engineering competition. The atmosphere was electric, with the clinking of glasses and the murmur of lively conversation providing the perfect backdrop for their creative brainstorming. As the two brilliant minds came together, a frantic scribbling on paper napkins began. They discussed their vision for a cutting-edge watch case, sleek and sturdy, crafted from unbreakable plastic using injection molding. And the movement? It would be cleverly mounted from the top and built straight into the case with ultrasonic welding. Everything would have to be sealed to minimize the use of screws and make the watch waterproof. The use of plastic was a perfect idea—it would limit the number of parts needed (only 51 instead of the usual 100 or so). This would also enable large-scale automation.

This was the sketch now in Ernst Thomke's hands. Mock knew that the only thing to save him from immediate dismissal for ordering the exorbitantly priced injection molding machine would be to convince his boss that this was the solution to his seemingly insuperable engineering challenge (Figure 3.2).

As Mock explained his and Müller's innovative idea, Thomke's eyes remained fixed on the sketch before him. Despite his initial frustration, the design caught his attention. He could feel a shift—this was something different. For over a year, he had been searching for an original idea that could deliver a high-quality yet affordable Swiss-made watch. Now, as he studied the sketch, he sensed he had found it. The meeting ended on a completely different note than it had begun. Thomke, now engaged, discussed the potential of this plastic watch with a newfound interest. And Mock, who had walked in expecting to lose his job, left with a newfound sense of purpose and validation. He and Jacques Müller were given 6 months to make it happen. Notwithstanding the excitement they felt, they were perhaps slightly concerned about needing a bit more time.

So, with the Swiss watch industry grappling with the existential threat posed by longstanding issues and the rise of quartz technology, the stage

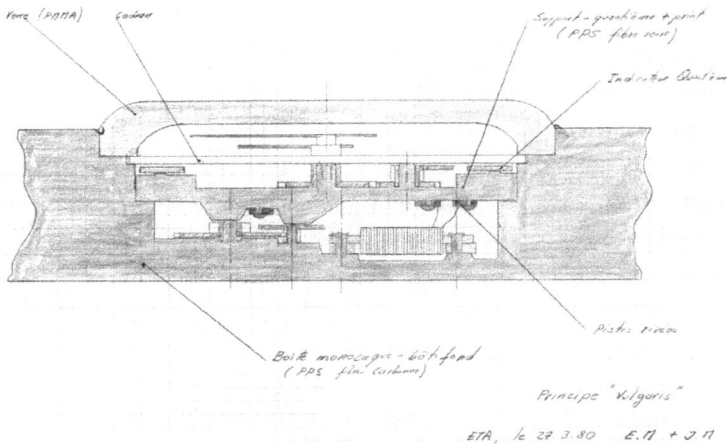

Figure 3.2 The first-ever sketch of the Swatch "Vulgaris" case, drawn on March 27, 1980. The sketch was part of the Schmid & Müller collection, auctioned by Sotheby's in Geneva in 2015

Source: Image courtesy of Sotheby's.

was now set for a turnaround. Amid the turmoil of restructuring and financial woes, a team of visionary engineers quietly laid the groundwork for a breakthrough that would reshape the industry.

Fuelled by the urgency to survive, Ernst Thomke's drive for innovation, and the ingenuity of Elmar Mock and Jacques Müller, the seeds of the Swatch were sown. Their collaboration and determination became the catalyst for a bold transformation as they set out to create the "cheapest and best watch of all time."

However, as they set out to bring the Swatch to the world and transform Swiss watchmaking, an understanding arose that having a superior product or state-of-the-art technology was insufficient. Effective marketing would be equally essential for success. Thomke knew that no matter how innovative or superior a product may be, its value would remain unrealized without effective promotion and communication.

He needed a bridge between the product and its audience, the narration of its value proposition in a compelling manner. Creation of this awareness was required quickly, to generate interest and drive customer purchases, ultimately translating product potential into tangible results.

Thomke knew that from identifying the right target audiences and crafting persuasive messaging, to leveraging the best channels for maximum exposure, effective marketing was demanded to ensure that the Swatch would be a success.

Thomke realized that while innovation may create the product, it is marketing that would bring it to life, thereby propelling it toward success in the marketplace. And he had set his eyes on global success. So he turned his attention to building a marketing strategy for Swatch and assembling a dedicated team for this purpose.

Commentary and Managerial Insights

Embrace Change and Innovation

> *Innovation is seeing what everybody has seen and thinking what nobody has thought.*
>
> —Dr. Albert Szent-Györgyi

The Swiss watchmakers' initial resistance to quartz technology highlights the dangers of clinging to tradition in the face of innovation. Businesses must continuously evolve and adapt to new technologies and market trends to stay competitive. In the late 1970s and early 1980s, the Swiss watch industry faced a crisis as it struggled to adapt to the emergence of quartz technology. This shift, initially dismissed by Swiss watchmakers as a passing fad, clearly revolutionized the industry. The reluctance to embrace quartz watches nearly led to the collapse of a sector that had been synonymous with precision and quality for centuries.

This underscores for business managers the importance of fostering a culture of innovation and adaptability. They should encourage their teams to explore new technologies and be open to rethinking established practices. Innovation should not be viewed as a threat but, rather, as an opportunity for growth and differentiation. Regularly assessing the market landscape and investing in research and development can help businesses stay ahead of the curve.

Several companies across various industries have faced similar challenges to the Swiss watch industry, clasping on to tradition instead of embracing innovation.

Consider Kodak, for example, a household name in photography for most of the twentieth century. It provides a striking example of what happens when a company fails to adapt to technological advances. Despite inventing the first digital camera in 1975, Kodak's management was hesitant to pursue the technology, fearing it would cannibalize its lucrative film business. This hesitation allowed more agile competitors like Canon and Sony to dominate the digital photography market. By the time Kodak attempted to catch up, it was too late. The company filed for bankruptcy in 2012, a stark reminder of the dangers of ignoring disruptive technologies.

Similarly, in the early 2000s, Blockbuster had the opportunity to buy a fledgling Netflix for a paltry US$50 million (by today's terms) but declined the offer, believing their traditional rental model would be secure. As streaming technology advanced and consumer preferences shifted toward online content, Blockbuster's refusal to adapt led to its downfall. By 2010, the company had filed for bankruptcy, with Netflix emerging as a dominant force in home entertainment.

And what about Nokia's dominance in the mobile phone market during the late 1990s and early 2000s? While the company recognized the growing role of software, it struggled to adapt to the smartphone era. As Apple and Android devices redefined the industry with their powerful operating systems and expansive app ecosystems, Nokia remained focused on hardware and failed to build a compelling software experience. This misalignment led to a steep decline, culminating in the sale of its mobile phone division to Microsoft in 2013. Nokia's story serves as a reminder that recognizing technological shifts is not enough; companies must also act decisively to align with changing consumer behavior and industry dynamics.

Xerox, known for its photocopiers, had a pioneering research center, Xerox PARC, which developed many groundbreaking technologies, including the graphical user interface (GUI), the computer mouse, and Ethernet networking. However, Xerox's management failed to recognize the commercial potential of these technologies, remaining focused instead on its core copier business. This allowed companies like Apple and Microsoft to take the lead in personal computing by building on the GUI concept and delivering it to the mass market. Xerox's story demonstrates that inventing new technologies is not enough. Successful innovation also requires vision, integration, and strategic follow-through.

What can today's managers learn from these cautionary tales?

First, managers should actively encourage exploration and experimentation. They should try to create an environment where employees feel both safe and empowered to explore new ideas and technologies without fear of failure; this can encourage cross-functional teams to collaborate and innovate.

Second, consistent investment in research and development (R&D) is needed. Allocating resources to R&D to stay ahead of technological trends can not only drive innovation but also prepare the company to pivot when necessary.

Third, managers should encourage regular market assessment within their organizations. Continuously monitoring the market landscape for emerging trends and technologies can be critical, and being proactive rather than reactive can even provide a competitive edge and a first-mover advantage.

Fourth, embracing change management when needed can be essential. Developing robust change management processes can help an organization adapt smoothly to new technologies and business practices.

Finally, leveraging customer feedback can be crucial to any business. Regularly gathering and analyzing customer input to understand evolving needs and preferences can guide innovation and ensure that new technologies align with market demands.

The launch of the Swatch serves as a quintessential example of how fostering a culture of innovation and adaptability can help businesses avoid the pitfalls experienced by companies like Kodak, Blockbuster, Nokia, and Xerox.

Thomke was able to create an environment that actively encouraged exploration and experimentation. His internal competition challenged engineers to think outside the box to develop a cost-effective yet high-quality watch. This culture of innovation allowed Mock and Müller to explore radical new ideas. The freedom to experiment was instrumental in transforming a bold concept into a groundbreaking product.

Despite financial turmoil, resources were also allocated to developing new technologies and materials. The investment in an injection molding machine, although initially regarded as somewhat crazy and controversial, enabled the production of plastic watches that were not only cost-effective but also innovative.

This commitment to experimentation and R&D allowed Swatch to stay ahead of technological trends and pivot effectively in response to market changes. The team behind Swatch was able to recognize the failure of traditional Swiss watchmakers to compete with the quartz technology championed by Japanese firms.

With a holistic understanding of the market landscape, they identified a niche for a stylish, mass-produced watch that could appeal to a broader audience. Such a proactive approach ensured that Swatch was not just reactive but also strategically positioned to meet emerging trends.

The restructure of the Swiss watch industry, including the merger of ASUAG and SSIH, exemplifies effective change management. Nicolas Hayek's leadership in overseeing this merger involved comprehensive change management processes, including restructuring operations, integrating new technologies, and shifting strategic focus. By managing these changes effectively, Swatch was able to transition from traditional watchmaking practices to innovative, modern production techniques.

Swatch's story is also a reminder that crises can be powerful catalysts for change and innovation. The country's watch industry's near-collapse forced it to rethink its strategies and ultimately led to the creation of something groundbreaking. The financial troubles of ASUAG and SSIH during the quartz crisis were a turning point for the Swiss watch industry. Instead of succumbing to the fear of collapse, they used the crisis as an impetus to innovate and restructure.

Business managers are encouraged to view crises not merely as threats, but as opportunities to reassess, adapt and innovate. In challenging times, companies should foster creative thinking and remain open to bold change. This mindset can help businesses emerge stronger and more resilient.

Of course, this may require taking risks and the support of bold, unconventional ideas. Mock's decision to order an injection molding machine without authorization was a daring move that could have cost him his job. However, his vision for a plastic watch was exactly the innovative idea the company needed. And of course, Thomke's ability to recognize the potential in Mock's idea and support it was also crucial. We will see later that much of Swatch's marketing strategy was a collection of daring and unconventional ideas.

For business leaders, fostering an environment where employees feel empowered to take risks is vital. This involves providing support for original ideas and understanding that not all risks will pay off. Celebrating both successes and failures as learning opportunities can encourage a culture of innovation to drive the company forward.

The Swiss watch industry in the 1980s also provides a great example of the importance of pivoting for adaptation and survival; it demonstrates how to capitalize on emergent market opportunities. There are many examples of companies around the world that have had to reinvent themselves in order to prosper.

Nintendo, originally a playing card company founded in 1889, transitioned into electronic gaming in the 1970s and emerged as a market leader by 1983 with the launch of the Famicom, later known internationally as the Nintendo Entertainment System (NES).

Another example is PayPal, originally conceived as a way for moving money between Palm Pilots. In 1999–2000, the company shifted its initial focus to become one of the world's leading online payment platforms. By adapting to the growing demand for online payments and e-commerce, PayPal expanded its services to facilitate transactions on websites and mobile apps, transforming how people send and receive money digitally.

Then there is Burbn, originally a location-based check-in app, which, in 2010, morphed into Instagram. This rebranded app moved its focus to be exclusively on photo- and video-sharing, in response to user feedback and market trends. By simplifying its features and emphasizing visual content, Instagram quickly gained traction to become a ubiquitous social media platform, eventually being acquired by Facebook for its innovative approach to mobile and video photography, as well as its related novel approach to social networking.

An additional example is provided by Stanley, the renowned manufacturer of insulated drinking bottles, tumblers, and mugs. The company's history can be traced back to 1913 when William Stanley Jr. invented the first vacuum-insulated steel bottle. For nearly a century, Stanley primarily targeted a male demographic with their classic designs. However, in 2020, facing stagnant growth, Stanley made a remarkable comeback through a user-generated content viral marketing campaign on TikTok. This strategic move resulted in a significant surge in sales, soaring from US$70 million to US$750 million by 2022. The once perceived "macho brand" transformed into a fashionable accessory available in a variety of colors and limited-edition versions, appealing to women seeking stylish and sustainable hydration solutions. The success of Stanley's transformation can be attributed to their gender awareness and adept utilization of social media.

These four cases highlight how companies can successfully pivot in response to changing market dynamics, consumer preferences, and technological advancements. They demonstrate the importance of innovation and adaptability in sustaining long-term success.

Interestingly, current developments in the watch industry suggest that Swiss watchmakers may be lagging behind once again, by failing to keep up with the burgeoning smartwatch market. Today, Apple has emerged as one of the world's largest watch manufacturers, underscoring the Swiss industry's missed opportunity, reminiscent of their earlier oversight during the Quartz Revolution in the 1970s.

This reluctance to embrace technological change has cost Swiss watchmakers a substantial share in a rapidly growing segment. To catch up, the industry should consider innovating and integrating modern technology with traditional watchmaking excellence. Swiss brands could, for example, explore partnerships with tech companies to develop smartwatches that offer the elegance and quality expected from Swiss watches, combined with the functionality and connectivity of modern smartwatches. By leveraging their strong brand heritage and focusing on unique value propositions—such as superior craftsmanship, advanced materials, and exclusive designs—Swiss watchmakers could potentially carve out a niche in the smartwatch market.

Balance Technology and Market Focus

If a man has good corn, or wood, or boards, or pigs, to sell, or can make better chairs, or knives, crucibles, or church organs than any-body else, you will find a broad, hard-beaten road to his house, though it be in the woods.

—Ralph Waldo Emerson

Emerson's quote above fundamentally suggests that having a superior product alone is enough to attract customers. While this idea emphasizes the importance of quality and excellence, it overlooks critical aspects of modern business success, particularly the necessity of a market orientation alongside a product or technology orientation.

The development of the Swatch watch was not only about creating a high-quality, innovative product; it was also about understanding the market's demand for affordable, fashionable, and reliable watches. It is not sufficient for companies just to innovate. They also need to ensure that their innovations meet market needs and preferences by adopting a market orientation. The Swatch story exemplifies how this dual approach can lead to groundbreaking success, demonstrating that even the best products require market fit to truly thrive.

A technology orientation refers to a company's strategic focus on and commitment to integrating new technologies into its business processes, products, and marketing efforts. It is a proactive attitude and strategic approach a company can adopt toward embracing and leveraging new technologies, and it usually involves a focus on developing and adopting cutting-edge technologies, investing significantly in R&D to drive technological advancements, an understanding of technological trends and market preferences, and building a culture that supports innovation. The benefits typically associated with a technology orientation include first-mover advantages, learning-curve effects, efficiency gains, customer experience benefits, market responsiveness, and revenue growth.

The Swatch story is a reminder of what makes technology successful: strong, supportive leadership, a clear technological vision aligned with company goals, a culture of creativity, and clinical attention to detail. The smooth integration of new technologies into existing processes through training, infrastructure upgrades, and workflow changes only underpinned the favorable outcome.

History shows that sometimes groundbreaking innovations can emerge not from careful market analysis but from serendipitous discovery and technological experimentation.

Penicillin, discovered by Alexander Fleming in 1928, is one of the most famous examples of a breakthrough innovation that arose from unexpected circumstances. Fleming was experimenting with Staphylococcus bacteria when he noticed that a mold called *Penicillium notatum* had contaminated his petri dishes and killed the surrounding bacteria. This accidental discovery led to the development of antibiotics, revolutionizing medicine and saving countless lives. Penicillin's impact was enormous, despite any initial market research or assessment of its potential. Its success underscores the importance of scientific exploration and the potential for serendipitous discoveries to have profound implications.

The Post-it Note, now a ubiquitous office supply, is another classic example. It was invented by accident at 3M. In 1968, Dr. Spencer Silver was attempting to create a super-strong adhesive but, instead, developed a low-tack, reusable one. For years, Silver struggled to find a practical application for his discovery. It wasn't until 1974 that Art Fry, a colleague at 3M, realized the adhesive could be used to create bookmarks that would not damage pages. This idea evolved into the Post-it Note, which became a massive commercial success. The invention was not the result of market demand; rather, it was an innovative by-product from a seemingly failed experiment.

The microwave oven is another serendipitous invention. Percy Spencer, an engineer at Raytheon, discovered the cooking potential of microwaves in 1945 while working on radar technology. Spencer noticed that a candy bar in his pocket had melted when he was near an active radar set. Intrigued, he experimented further to find that microwaves could cook food quickly and efficiently. Despite any initial market research suggesting a demand for such a product, the microwave oven eventually became a household staple, transforming cooking practices worldwide.

Velcro, the omnipresent fastening system, was invented by Swiss engineer George de Mestral in 1941 after he noticed how burrs stuck to his dog's fur during a walk in the woods. Upon examining the burrs under a microscope, de Mestral saw that they had tiny hooks that clung to fabric. This observation led to the development of Velcro, which found applications in various industries, including in fashion, aerospace, and even medicine. The invention was not driven by market research—it was driven by curiosity and the desire to mimic nature's design.

X-rays were discovered by Wilhelm Conrad Röntgen in 1895 while experimenting with cathode rays. Röntgen noticed that a fluorescent screen in his lab began to glow even though it was shielded. This indicated the presence of an unknown form of radiation that could pass through solid objects. This accidental discovery revolutionized medical diagnostics, allowing doctors to see inside the human body without invasive surgery. The technology quickly became an indispensable tool in medicine, despite any prior indication of its market potential.

These famous examples illustrate that while strategic planning and market assessment are vital for sustained business success, there is also significant value in fostering an environment that encourages exploration and experimentation. Serendipitous discoveries often arise from a culture of curiosity and a willingness to experiment without immediate concern for commercial outcomes.

However, there is arguably a good reason why the examples cited above have become timeless industry classics. It's because they are rare. While commercial success can sometimes purely be the result of technological exploration and experimentation, this tends to be more the exception than the rule. Therefore, to harness the power of a strong technology orientation—and to increase its chances of commercial success—a company should also complement it with a solid market orientation. What does that entail in practice?

A company that is market-oriented tends to carry out three processes very effectively: (1) intelligence generation, (2) intelligence dissemination, and (3) responsiveness to intelligence.

Intelligence generation involves tapping the market systematically and continuously, to generate strategically useful information about customers, competitors, and collaborators. There are different means through which this can be achieved, including secondary sources, (such as reports, existing studies, databases, and records), commissioning of market research (e.g., of intermediaries and consumers), and benchmarking and competitive intelligence (e.g., reverse engineering).

A powerful method for generating market intelligence is customer observation and ethnographic market research (i.e., observing and interacting with people in their natural environments to gain a deeper understanding of their behaviors, needs, and motivations) as these can be essential tools to uncover needs customers do not realize that they have. Sometimes, the most effective marketing is carried out away from the office, and as close to these customers as possible.

Second, generating a lot of information is useless unless that information reaches the right people at the right time. Thus, it is important for the organization to develop some strong interfunctional coordination as well. Anything that helps connect people within the organization, whether formally or informally, can help intelligence dissemination—for example, cross-functional teams, job rotations, internal reporting and documentation, intranets, and other communication technologies. The crucial point is that like intelligence generation, these should not be one-off activities. The intelligence dissemination must take place continuously in the background and should become part of the organizational culture.

Despite the significant financial investments that companies make in formal methods of disseminating information within their organizations, such as Customer Relationship Management (CRM) systems, intranet portals, internal newsletters, team meetings, and town halls, it is often the more informal means that prove to be most valuable.

The creation of the Swatch brand, for example, would not have been possible without two ETA engineers meeting up in a German pub for a drink! Studies in organizational psychology and communication have delved into the role of informal interactions in the workplace and their impact on outcomes such as creativity, collaboration, and knowledge-sharing. This body of research has uncovered what is popularly called the "water-cooler effect."

In a seminal 1973 research paper, sociologist Mark Granovetter argued that weak ties—that is, connections between individuals who are not closely acquainted—play a crucial role in the diffusion of information and access to diverse perspectives. These weak ties enhance individuals' social capital and network reach, facilitating the flow of new information and opportunities across different social circles.

Further research has explored how informal interactions in the workplace contribute to the formation of weak ties and the exchange of tacit knowledge. Chance encounters and spontaneous and unsystematic conversations in shared spaces have been found to create opportunities for employees to share insights, seek advice, and learn from each other in a less regimented and less hierarchical setting, promoting open communication and idea exchange.

One of the reasons behind the modern proliferation of open-office layouts, communal spaces, and amenities like coffee stations or lounge areas in organizations is due to research on the impact of physical workspace design on informal interactions and knowledge-sharing. Simply put, these features can facilitate spontaneous interactions and serendipitous encounters among employees, promoting collaboration and creativity. These interactions without any deliberate design to them tend to occur around common areas like water coolers, break rooms, or cafeterias.

While seemingly trivial, these casual interactions can have a significant impact on generating innovation within an organization. And this is partly why many companies are keen for their employees to spend at least a few days in the office, or go on team development off-sites, even in a post-Covid19 world where remote work and online meetings have become the norm. Virtual connections do not appear to possess the same degree of conversational impact and social capital accumulation as a chat around the good-old office water cooler.

Third, it is not enough for an organization to generate and disseminate information within the business. It is equally important for the organization to respond to that market intelligence promptly and accurately. This might mean considering whether to enter a market, match a competitor's price cut, or launch a new promotional campaign in answer to changing customer preferences.

Responding to market intelligence does not necessarily mean that a company needs to react to everything that happens in its external environment. It might simply mean that the relevant information is considered and its potential impact on the business strategy assessed carefully. An action may or may not ensue; a company may choose not to do anything after having analyzed the intelligence generated. The most important thing is that there are ongoing processes in place to deal with the market intelligence that has been generated and disseminated.

We often think of marketing as something people with marketing job titles do, like brand managers designing advertising campaigns, social media strategies, or pricing incentives. But sometimes the best kind of marketing is executed by people who do not even realize (or may be even shocked to realize!) they are doing marketing.

Swatch is a good example as it demonstrates the adoption of a market orientation through application of intelligence generation, dissemination, and responsiveness. Until a formal marketing team was set up, and even afterwards, marketing at Swatch was diluted throughout the organization to be carried out often very effectively and unconsciously by people who were not marketers.

Thomke had his fingers firmly on the pulse of the watch market. He understood the growing consumer preference for affordable, reliable, and fashionable quartz watches. This proactive approach allowed him to identify critical market insights that highlighted the need for a major shift from traditional watchmaking to embrace new technologies and consumer trends.

Once this intelligence was gathered, Swatch excelled in intelligence dissemination. The creation of the Swatch was the result of strong cross-functional integration and collaboration between key people at ETA. It was the fusion of Thomke's vision about the market potential for a mass-market watch that was affordable and stylish, Mock's expertise in plastics, and Müller's deep knowledge of watch movements. These key ingredients and the water-cooler effect during the German training trip combined to create a revolutionary product. Then later, of course, the addition of marketing know-how would turn a good technology and product into a resonant brand and an exciting customer experience.

This alignment enabled cohesive efforts toward innovation, product development, and market development. Then Swatch demonstrated remarkable responsiveness to market intelligence, by quickly adapting its strategies and operations to capitalize on the opportunity, launching a product that was both technologically revolutionary and aligned with customer needs. Then the innovative use of plastic and simplified construction in the Swatch design not only reduced costs but also facilitated large-scale production, meeting the market's demand for affordability without sacrificing quality.

In summary, Swatch's success story highlights the crucial role of the fusion of technology and market orientations in business strategy. Through effective intelligence generation, dissemination, and responsiveness, Swatch not only navigated a period of industry crisis but also set a new standard for innovation and market adaptation. Of course, there are many other examples of companies that have achieved commercial success by merging technology and market orientations effectively.

Samsung, for example, combines its technological prowess with a keen understanding of consumer preferences to develop a wide range of electronic products. From smartphones and televisions to home appliances and semiconductors, Samsung leverages innovation and market research to create products that resonate with customers worldwide.

Adobe combines its expertise in software development with a market-oriented approach to deliver creative solutions for designers, artists, and businesses. By understanding the needs of creative professionals and businesses, the company innovates its software offerings to enable digital transformation to drive success in the creative economy.

Don't Just Lead, Transform

Management is doing things right; leadership is doing the right things.
—Peter Drucker

Strong leadership and a clear vision are essential for navigating through crises and driving transformation. Leaders must be able to inspire and guide their teams toward a common goal. Thomke's leadership and vision were critical for the success of the Swatch project. And later, Hayek's contribution and steer would also become instrumental in continuing the turnaround of the Swiss watch industry and the growth of Swatch Group.

Managers can learn from this by understanding the transformational importance of strategic leadership and its capacity for inspiring others. But what is transformational leadership exactly?

Transformational leadership is a style that aims to inspire positive changes in individuals and organizations by motivating others to pursue shared goals and realize their full potential. It is commonly understood to include four core dimensions:

- Idealized Influence—involves leaders serving as role models to gain the trust and respect of their followers.
- Inspirational motivation—entails leaders inspiring to galvanize their followers through the generation of a compelling vision of the future.
- Intellectual stimulation—involves encouraging creativity, innovation, and critical thinking among followers.
- Individual consideration—refers to leaders providing personalized support, coaching, and mentoring to meet the individual needs of their followers.

Research has shown that transformational leadership is associated with many positive outcomes such as increased job satisfaction, organizational commitment, employee motivation, and performance. Additionally, transformational leadership has been linked to promoting organizational development by fostering a shared vision, commitment to goals, higher levels of morality and employee motivation. The effectiveness of transformational leadership lies in its ability to create trust between leaders and followers, encouraging employees to go beyond their formal roles and obligations. Charismatic leadership is also a key attribute of transformational leadership, and it has been identified as a significant predictor of how leaders perform.

In summary, transformational leadership builds trust, inspires ambition, promotes innovation, and supports individual growth. By embodying these traits, transformational leaders help organizations navigate complexity, embrace change, and achieve sustained success.

Thomke exemplified these principles. His idealized influence was evident in his role as a model of innovation and resilience. Amid the quartz crisis, his commitment to reviving the Swiss watch industry earned him the trust and respect of his team. His launch of an internal design competition demonstrated belief in his employees' potential and his willingness to lead by example. He inspired them with a bold and clear vision: to create the "cheapest and best watch of all time," made entirely in Switzerland.

This ambitious goal motivated the engineers to think creatively and work tirelessly. His reaction to the plastic watch sketch presented by Elmar Mock—transforming initial anger into excitement and support—demonstrated his own ability to pivot his emotions to then inspire his team even in challenging situations.

He also encouraged intellectual stimulation by fostering an environment where creativity and innovation were valued, as exemplified again by the design competition he launched. Even when initial attempts fell short, Thomke maintained high expectations and continued to challenge his team, ultimately leading to the breakthrough idea of the Swatch.

Finally, Thomke demonstrated individual consideration by recognizing and supporting the unique talents of his team members. When Mock presented his plastic watch concept, Thomke listened and saw its potential, despite his initially unorthodox approach. He provided Mock and Müller the time and resources needed to develop their idea, demonstrating his commitment to nurturing individual talents and fostering personal growth.

Jim Collins, in his book *Good to Great*, offers a parallel framework. He identifies a specific type of leadership, which he terms "Level 5 Leadership," as a key factor in the transformation from good to great. "Level 5" leaders bring a paradoxical blend of personal humility and professional will. They are modest and unpretentious and, at the same time, possess an intense determination to do whatever it takes to make the company successful.

The fact that the birth of the Swatch is often associated in popular culture with leaders that have come after him (such as Nicolas Hayek) is testament to Thomke's humility. He was committed to the long-term success of the company, laying the groundwork for his successors, and harnessing technology as an accelerator.

In addition, using a great analogy by Collins, Thomke prioritized "getting the right people on the bus" (and the wrong people off the bus) before deciding on the direction to drive it. In other words, it was important for him to have the right team in place before making strategic decisions.

The business world offers many other examples of transformational leadership. Jack Welch, as CEO of GE, implemented Six Sigma and bold restructuring measures that elevated the company to unprecedented heights. Satya Nadella, at Microsoft, ushered in a cultural and strategic shift from legacy software to a cloud-first, mobile-first model, revitalizing innovation and organizational agility. His emphasis on empathy, inclusion, and a growth mindset empowered employees to embrace change and positioned Microsoft as a renewed leader in the tech space. Indra Nooyi, at PepsiCo, led with vision and social responsibility. Her "Performance with Purpose" initiative aligned health, profitability, and sustainability, and her inclusive leadership style drove cultural transformation across the company.

The concept of visionary leadership advanced by management scholars Westley and Mintzberg is also useful to study the senior leadership of Swatch in the early 1980s. These scholars observed that only at the right time, with the right leader and the right audience, can strategy transform into vision and leadership become visionary. According to them, visionary leadership manifests in different ways, shaped by the challenges leaders face and the qualities they bring to their roles. Despite these variations, what unites them is an ability to inspire and propel their organizations toward an ambitious future.

Some, like Steve Jobs at Apple, possess an almost evangelical determination to realize the potential of their products. While they may not always be the original inventors, they articulate their vision with such conviction that they rally teams and customers alike, transforming ideas into movements. Others, such as Edward Land of Polaroid, are driven by a singular moment of inspiration—an original and holistic vision that consumes them, pushing innovation forward with relentless intensity.

Then there are leaders whose visionary approach is deeply rooted in adaptability and pragmatism. Lee Iacocca, who steered Ford and Chrysler through pivotal transformations, exemplified this. He possessed a keen ability to read situations, recognize critical success factors, and bring people together to execute a vision that was as strategic as it was forward-thinking.

Some visionaries are not fixated on a singular product or outcome; instead, they focus on the underlying processes that shape success. Jan

Carlzon at SAS, for example, famously prioritized customer experience and operational insight over traditional corporate hierarchies, demonstrating how vision can be as much about structure and culture as it is about innovation.

Regardless of their specific approach, visionary leaders share an unshakable belief in what is possible. Whether through innovation, persuasion, adaptability, or insight, they can reshape industries and redefine the future. However, as Westley and Mintzberg caution, visionary leadership is not always synonymous with effective leadership. Many of these leaders, despite their inspiring qualities, can be challenging to work with. Their relentless pursuit of a vision often comes with interpersonal and organizational friction, underscoring the reality that transformational leadership is as much about execution as it is about inspiration.

In this regard, Thomke's leadership at Swatch exemplified the qualities of a visionary driven by originality and a profound moment of insight. His vision was not merely to produce another watch but to redefine the very essence of Swiss watchmaking. He envisioned an affordable, high-quality Swiss watch, which broke away from the industry's traditional focus on exclusivity and luxury. And his vision extended beyond the product itself. With his marketing team, he sought to shift consumer perceptions and disrupt the dynamics of an industry that had long been resistant to change. Eventually, his leadership would be not only about invention but also about rethinking how an industry could operate.

Sources and Further Readings

Atuahene-Gima, K., and A. Ko. 2001. "An Empirical Investigation of the Effect of Market Orientation and Entrepreneurship Orientation Alignment on Product Innovation." *Organization Science* 12 (1): 54–74.

Auh, S., and O. Merlo. 2012. "The Power of Marketing Within the Firm: Its Contribution to Business Performance and the Effect of Power Asymmetry." *Industrial Marketing Management* 41 (5): 861–873.

Beer, M., and N. Nohria. 2000. "Cracking the Code of Change." *Harvard Business Review* 78 (3): 133–141.

Boin, A., A. McConnell, and P. Hart. 2010. *Governing After Crisis.* Cambridge University Press.

Christensen, C. M., and M. Overdorf. 2000. "Meeting the Challenge of Disruptive Change." *Harvard Business Review* 78 (2): 66–76.

Collins, J. 2001. *Good to Great: Why Some Companies Make the Leap... and Others Don't.* HarperCollins.

Gittell, J. H. 2001. "Investing in Relationships." *Harvard Business Review* 79 (6): 28–30.

Granovetter, M. 1973. "The Strength of Weak Ties." *American Journal of Sociology* 78 (6): 1360–1380.

Greyser, S. A. 2009. "Corporate Brand Reputation and Brand Crisis Management." *Management Decision* 47 (4): 590–602.

Han, J. K., N. Kim, and R. K. Srivastava. 1998. "Market Orientation and Organizational Performance: Is Innovation a Missing Link?" *Journal of Marketing* 62 (4): 30–45.

Homburg, C., and C. Pfelesser. 2000. "A Multiple-Layer Model of Market-Oriented Organizational Culture: Measurement Issues and Performance Outcomes." *Journal of Marketing Research* 37 (4): 449–462.

Jaworski, B. J., and A. K. Kohli. 1993. "Market Orientation: Antecedents and Consequences." *Journal of Marketing* 57 (3): 53–70.

Kirca, A. H., S. Jayachandran, and W. O. Bearden. 2005. "Market Orientation: A Meta-Analytic Review and Assessment of Its Antecedents and Impact on Performance." *Journal of Marketing* 69 (2): 1–14.

Kohli, A. K., and B. J. Jaworski. 1990. "Market Orientation: The Construct, Research Propositions, and Managerial Implications." *Journal of Marketing* 54 (2): 1–18.

Laird, D., and L. D. McLean. 2005. "Organizational Culture's Influence on Creativity and Innovation: A Review of the Literature and Implications for Human Resource Development." *Advances in Developing Human Resources* 7 (2): 151–159.

Langerak, F., E. J. Hultink, and H. S. J. Robben. 2004. "The Impact of Market Orientation, Product Advantage, and Launch Proficiency on New Product Performance and Organizational Performance." *Journal of Product Innovation Management* 21 (2): 79–94.

Merlo, O., and S. Auh. 2009. "The Effects of Entrepreneurial Orientation, Market Orientation, and Marketing Subunit Influence on Firm Performance." *Marketing Letters* 20 (3): 295–311.

Mitroff, I., P. Shrivastava, and E. Firdaus. 1987. "Effective Crisis Management." *The Academy of Management Executive* 1 (4): 283–292.

Reichers, A. E., J. P. Wanous, and J. T. Austin. 1997. "Understanding and Managing Cynicism About Organizational Change." *Academy of Management Executive* 11 (1): 48–59.

Slater, S. F., and J. C. Narver. 1998. "Customer-Led and Market-Oriented: Let's Not Confuse the Two." *Strategic Management Journal* 19: 1001–1006.

Westley, F., and H. Mintzberg. 1989. "Visionary Leadership and Strategic Management." *Strategic Management Journal* 10 (S1): 17–32.

CHAPTER 4

First Steps Against the Clock

Initially, manufacturing the Swatch was an uphill battle, fraught with seemingly insurmountable obstacles. The team behind the watch faced challenges at every turn—the hands would run backward, or sometimes not move at all. For 15 arduous months, they struggled to create a working prototype, pouring blood, sweat, and tears into their creation. But even after the prototype was finally complete, the struggles continued. By late 1981, they had managed to produce only five watches, which were plagued with issues, only working for just five days before breaking down.

However, just when all seemed lost, breakthroughs started happening, partly thanks to support from external sources. For example, the Swatch team was able to perfect the quality of the plastic with support from Lego, a company with vast expertise in handling plastic materials.

Shortly before Christmas 1981, the team finally overcame the remaining challenges. They watched their creation take shape, a reflection of their persistence and hard work. By the following year, the new watch was already being tested in the American market—though, as we will see, with mixed results.

In 1981, Thomke, Mock, and Müller only had one goal: to create an affordable watch and challenge Asian manufacturers. Initially, marketing was not a consideration. Their focus was on producing a 100 percent Swiss-made watch with production costs under CHF 10. This was an ambitious idea amid the intricacy, tradition, and high costs of the Swiss watch industry.

In time, this simple, inexpensive plastic watch would challenge industry conventions and redefine perceptions of Swiss watches. More than just a watch, Swatch became an expression of accessibility, proving that quality watches weren't solely for the elite. With its vibrant colors and playful designs, it brought a sense of fun to timekeeping and resonated with a broad audience. Beyond being a successful product, Swatch played a key role in revitalizing the Swiss watch industry, marking the beginning of a new chapter in its history.

The turnaround of the Swiss watch industry was not solely the result of individual leadership or the Swatch's market disruption; it was also underpinned by critical structural reforms and operational innovations. A decisive factor was the consolidation of ASUAG and SSIH into a unified entity, eventually rebranded as SMH and, later, the Swatch Group. This merger—orchestrated with the support of Swiss banks—centralized decision making and enabled the rationalization of production systems. By consolidating what had previously been a fragmented manufacturing process—most notably centralizing movement production at ETA—the industry reduced costs and achieved economies of scale, allowing Swiss watchmakers to compete more effectively with Japanese mass production. The adoption of vertical integration further enhanced supply chain control and cost efficiency, stabilizing the financial health of the industry and laying the groundwork for large-scale innovations, such as the Swatch itself.

In addition to operational efficiencies, the restructuring extended to the workforce. By integrating previously dispersed operations, the Swiss watch industry overcame inefficiencies that had long hindered its competitiveness. This strategic consolidation provided the financial and organizational backbone necessary for innovative products like the Swatch to succeed.

Moreover, the emphasis on precision engineering remained critical. Rather than solely pivoting to quartz watches, the Swiss watch industry leveraged its expertise in high-quality mechanical movements. By doing so, it retained a foothold in the luxury market, positioning itself as a leader in both tradition and modernity. These systemic foundations ensured that the industry was not only capable of recovering from its crisis but could also be resilient in the face of future challenges.

Yet, alongside these structural reforms and operational innovations, there was another indispensable ingredient that played a pivotal role in Swatch's success: a masterful marketing strategy. This strategy needed to do more than just sell watches—it had to captivate the imagination, inspire desire, and create a movement. By invoking all the senses and connecting with audiences through compelling storytelling, emotional resonance, and a bold, unconventional narrative style, the marketing approach transformed Swatch from a product into a cultural phenomenon. Without this crucial element, even the most innovative of products might have failed to reach its full potential.

Thomke was not a marketer, so his initial thoughts in this domain were rather limited, focused primarily on devising a temporary name for the secret project that would eventually become the Swatch. One day, inspiration struck. It came in the form of the Delirium watch, with its innovative technology that integrated the movement directly into the watch case. Thomke landed on a name that he thought might capture the attention of the masses: "Delirium vulgare," a Latin phrase evoking a Delirium watch for the common people. However, Thomke knew that he needed more than just a brand name. That's where Franz Sprecher, a seasoned marketing consultant, came in.

When Sprecher joined the team, he was met with a plain black prototype bearing the Delirium Vulgare brand name. He was underwhelmed to say the least. It was clear to him that this would not be enough to surpass Japanese competitors. Sprecher recognized the need to elevate the product from a simple inexpensive commodity to a captivating brand.

Thus, the Swatch brand name was born. It was a brilliant idea—catchy and distinctive, encapsulating the essence of the product (whether it be sporty, secondary, or Swiss!) in a single word. With this new name, the Swatch began to transcend beyond just being a watch; it slowly transformed into an experience, an emotion, or a statement. Gradually, the notion of a fashion accessory that tells time gained momentum. Sprecher created slogans like "You don't wear the same tie every day, do you?" to convey the idea that the Swatch was a fashion accessory that ticks.

However, Thomke and Sprecher knew that this brand narrative would only work if supported by outstanding design. So, in late 1981, Thomke also hired two brilliant designers—Marlyse Schmid and Bernard Müller (Jacques Müller's brother)—to bring the brand vision to life.

Schmid and Müller's creative minds were instrumental in shaping the iconic visual identity of Swatch. With their keen eye for detail and finger on the pulse of pop culture and fashion trends, they were one of the driving forces behind Swatch's unique and captivating designs in the first

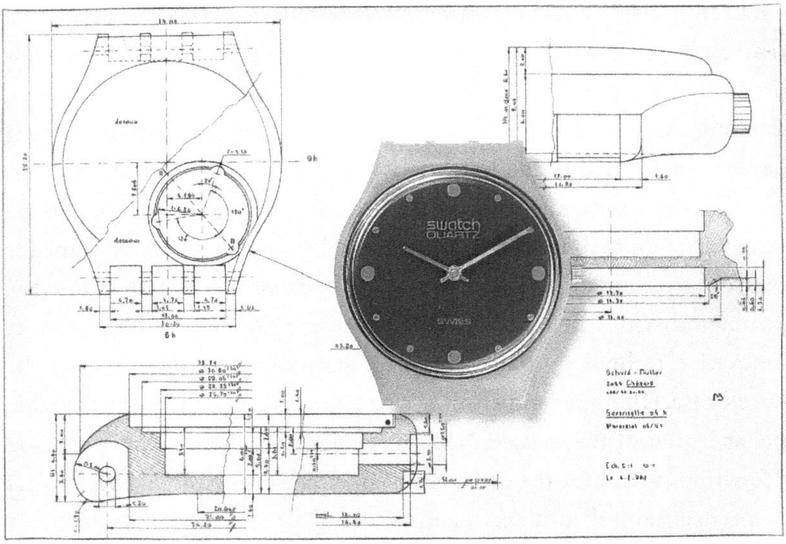

Figure 4.1 An early Swatch design by Schmid & Müller, part of the Schmid & Müller collection auctioned by Sotheby's in Geneva in 2015

Source: Image courtesy of Sotheby's.

few months. They poured their souls into every aspect of the brand, from the logo to the case design, and every other artistic element of this process (Figure 4.1).

Another driving force behind Swatch's positioning as fashionable was designer Jean Robert, who was engaged in the summer of 1983. Robert was born in La Chaux-de-Fonds—the center of Swiss watch industry. After training as an engraver, he worked as a graphic designer at Pirelli in Milan and later at Pentagram Design Studio in London. In 1977, he and his wife Käti Durrer settled in Zurich.

With his design concepts, Robert helped Swatch achieve resounding success. He worked on dial designs, packaging, and the presentation in the salesrooms. The first 350 models, from 1983 to 1989, bear his signature and sold over 100 million units. Ernst Thomke today still maintains that "Jean Robert made a huge difference. He changed our whole attitude. He convinced us to dare to do something."

At the end of 1982, with the basics of the product, design, and brand strategies in place, Thomke then hired Konstantin Theile to design and execute the rest of the sales and marketing strategy for Swatch. Theile, with a PhD in economics and a background in the banking and pharmaceutical industries, was a versatile professional with a strong ambition to lead. His thirst for something new and exciting led him to the world of watches when one of his university professors mentioned an opportunity at ETA. Despite having limited knowledge of the industry, Theile wasn't afraid to take risks and joined ETA on September 1, 1982, and was made responsible for sales and marketing of watch movements in South America, the Middle East, India, and Africa.

However, Theile soon realized that he was responsible for less than 1 percent of the company's turnover, and he often humorously introduced himself as a "Mickey Mouse director" of the firm. This realization did not align with his ambitious nature, and after just 3 months, he knew the job was not for him. When Theile entered Thomke's office with his resignation letter, little did he know that he would leave with a new job title.

Thomke had been searching for a Head of Marketing and Sales for Swatch, but skepticism ran deep within ETA. With the company facing financial difficulties, few saw potential in the project, and no one wanted the job. Theile likely secured the role not for his marketing expertise but because he was the only one willing to take it. Young and inexperienced, he knew little about the watch industry. Yet, while he may have lacked experience, he made up for it with determination—embracing bold risks and exploring uncharted territory.

What Thomke valued most about Theile was his international experience and perspective, both personally and professionally. For Swatch to succeed globally, it needed a marketing leader with an international mindset. Despite his lack of experience in the watch industry, Theile threw himself into the role of marketing director with dedication. In his first few months, he worked long hours—often 16 to 18 hours a day—balancing a full schedule of meetings from 9 a.m. to 5 p.m. while continuing to develop ideas well into the evening. His first task was no small challenge: It involved not only testing and refining existing ideas but also bringing fresh thinking to a sustainable international marketing strategy.

The brand name was the first thing he gave his attention to. If Swatch was going to be globally recognized, then he had to make sure, without any doubt, that the brand name worked equally well in different languages and across cultures. But with no budget for a market research company and no benefit of the Internet, how could he possibly figure out, for example, whether Swatch had any negative connotations in different languages?

In the 1980s, marketers were absolutely petrified of making translation blunders. It was easy to do so; some of the errors made proved to be of near epic proportions—the stuff of legend. For example, the infamous Parker Pen slogan—"It won't leak in your pocket and embarrass you"—was translated into Spanish as "It won't leak in your pocket and make you pregnant." Electrolux, a Swedish home appliance manufacturer, ran an infamous marketing campaign in the United States with the slogan "Nothing sucks like an Electrolux," which was intended to convey the powerful suction of their vacuum cleaners but, unfortunately, resulted in something far less complimentary.

Theile's ingenious solution to the translation dilemma was uncomplicated yet effective. He obtained a copy of the telephone directory for Bern, which at the time would typically include a comprehensive list of numbers for individuals and organizations in the Canton. Theile swiftly located the section for embassies, dialing a multitude of numbers, eagerly awaiting a response. When someone answered, often with a distinct foreign accent, he politely greeted them and introduced himself before posing a crucial question: Did the word "Swatch" hold any offensive connotations in their native tongue? This creative solution to gather market research proved to be a lifesaver for the Swatch brand at a time when resources were incredibly limited. It serves as a powerful reminder that one doesn't always need outrageously complex market research; sometimes, it is simply a matter of being resourceful and creative.

As the Swatch team worked to bring their new watch to life, they encountered a series of challenges. From technical hurdles in manufacturing to the careful process of refining the product, progress required persistence. However, with determination and support from external partners like Lego, they gradually overcame these obstacles.

The launch of Swatch was not just a feat of engineering—it was also a reflection of the team's resilience and collaboration. As they marked their initial success, they knew their work was far from over. With the product and brand foundation in place, their focus shifted to the next crucial step:

assembling a dedicated marketing team to develop a strategy that would introduce Swatch to the world. This phase would play a defining role in shaping Swatch's future, built on creativity, innovation, resourcefulness, and the power of storytelling.

Commentary and Managerial Insights

Persevere, Guided by a Clear Vision

I have not failed. I've just found 10,000 ways that won't work.
—Thomas Edison

Perseverance and resilience are critical in the face of seemingly insurmountable challenges. The Swatch team faced numerous technical hurdles, including problems with how the watch hands moved and the prototypes breaking down. Despite these setbacks, they persisted for 15 months to create a working prototype. Their determination is a powerful reminder that success often demands patience, grit, and the ability to push through significant obstacles.

For business managers and entrepreneurs, this underscores the importance of maintaining resilience when faced with challenges. Building a successful product or business often involves navigating through periods of trial and error. Leaders should foster a culture that encourages persistence and views failures as learning opportunities rather than setbacks.

Perseverance and resilience are crucial qualities in the realm of business and entrepreneurship, offering potential advantages and disadvantages. On the positive side, individuals and organizations that exhibit perseverance and resilience are better equipped to navigate through challenges, setbacks, and uncertainties. They are more likely to stay committed to their goals, learn from failures, and adapt to changing circumstances, ultimately increasing their chances of long-term success.

Moreover, resilience can serve as a catalyst for entrepreneurial intentions, driving individuals to pursue opportunities even in the face of adversity. By fostering a culture that values persistence and views failures as learning experiences, leaders can create an environment where innovation and growth thrive.

However, there are also potential downsides to excessive perseverance. In some cases, individuals may persist in pursuing unviable ventures or strategies, leading to wasted resources and missed opportunities for redirection. This may lead to problems such as escalating commitment, a phenomenon where individuals continue to invest time, money, and effort into a failing course of action due to the amount already committed, often driven by the desire to avoid admitting failure. This behavior is akin to a gambler who continues to bet more money in an attempt to recover previous losses, ignoring the increasing risk and probability of further losses, and becoming trapped in a cycle of mounting investment and diminishing returns.

Moreover, excessive perseverance can lead to burnout. The relentless pursuit of a goal without adequate rest and reflection can exhaust physical and mental resources, diminishing productivity and creativity. People may become so fixated on an original path that they ignore valuable feedback or alternative solutions that could lead to success more efficiently.

Therefore, while resilience is important, recognizing the signs of diminishing returns and knowing when to pivot or abandon a course of action are also essential. Strategic flexibility—demonstrating the willingness to adapt and change direction based on new information or changing circumstances—is a critical complement to perseverance. It allows for a balanced approach where persistence is guided by practicality and responsiveness to the realities of the situation.

It is a common risk for management to become attached to unsuccessful projects. To avoid prolonging the life of failing ones, managers can try to cultivate an atmosphere of honesty, by promoting a culture where team members feel comfortable expressing any concerns or criticisms about the progress of an undertaking without the fear of reprisal or repercussion. Encouraging flexibility and adaptability, by being open to modifying or abandoning a project, if necessary, is also key. Recognizing when an endeavor is not effective and being receptive to other alternatives can prove vital. And a process for review and feedback should be implemented; it is recommended that teams be made up of people with varying levels of enthusiasm for the project, so that tough questions may also be asked.

While resilience and perseverance come with their own inherent risks, if there is a well-grounded belief, a vision, and an original market insight at the heart of the product design, then the risks may be worthwhile. The development of the Swatch was driven by the vision of Thomke and his team, who believed that the Swiss watch industry could be revitalized by transforming the watch into a fashion statement and making it affordable without compromising on quality.

This belief was crucial in driving the innovation process, despite widespread skepticism and criticism from colleagues and industry experts who doubted the feasibility of such a radical shift. They maintained a steadfast belief in their strategy and continued to push forward despite the negativity, as they understood there was a customer problem to be solved. The Swatch team's ability to combine resilience with market awareness was instrumental to the product's eventual success.

Steve Jobs is often cited as a visionary leader who saw opportunities and potential in technology that others initially overlooked. Persisting in his vision was crucial for him, because he had unique insights into consumer desires and the potential of integrated technology that others initially overlooked. Jobs understood that technology should be intuitive and emotionally engaging, prioritizing user-friendly interfaces and elegant designs to create deeper connections with consumers. He also recognized the power of seamlessly integrating hardware and software to ensure consistent quality and performance, contrasting sharply with the industry trend of specializing in one or the other.

Anticipating future market needs, Jobs foresaw the potential of personal computing for everyday people and the convergence of digital devices into a cohesive ecosystem, exemplified by products like the iPod, iPhone, and iPad. His belief in creating entirely new product categories and maintaining high standards of quality, despite skepticism, led to groundbreaking innovations that transformed industries and set new benchmarks. Jobs' ability to see that technology could be both powerful and user-friendly, coupled to his relentless pursuit of this vision, established strong brand loyalty and differentiated Apple from its competitors, proving the profound impact of his foresight and resilience.

The business world is full of other stories of resilience and visionary leadership. For example, in Amazon's early days, Jeff Bezos faced skepticism about the viability of online retailing, the sustainability of his business model prioritizing customer experience over short-term profits, and the long-term potential of his vision for Amazon's expansion beyond books. Despite initial doubts, Bezos remained committed to his vision of offering a superior customer experience, fast delivery, easy returns, and personalized recommendations. Amazon's relentless focus on customer satisfaction and innovation has since proven skeptics wrong, and drastically so, establishing the company as a global e-commerce powerhouse.

Reed Hastings, cofounder of Netflix, faced criticism in the early days of the company for its innovative subscription model for DVD rentals, which was seen as a threat to traditional video rental stores like Blockbuster. As Netflix transitioned to streaming media, those lacking his conviction questioned the company's ability to secure content rights. Additionally, Hastings's decision to invest in original content production was met with doubt. Yet his commitment to innovation and investment in original content has proven critics wrong, establishing the company as a global leader in digital entertainment.

Bill Gates, cofounder of Microsoft, recognized the potential for personal computing to be transformational at a time when computers were primarily seen as business tools. Gates envisioned a future where every home and office would have a personal computer. He acted on this vision by developing user-friendly software that made computing accessible to the masses. His focus on creating an operating system that could run on a variety of hardware platforms was a key insight that set Microsoft apart. This approach allowed Microsoft to dominate the software market, providing the backbone for a personal computing revolution.

After initially facing criticism and cynicism, Larry Page and Sergey Brin, the cofounders of Google, exhibited resilience in the face of disbelief as they revolutionized the way information is accessed and organized on the Internet with their innovative search engine. Developing their algorithm, PageRank, at a time when existing search engines struggled to deliver relevant results, Page and Brin prioritized webpages based on their importance and interconnections. This unique approach quickly established Google as the dominant search engine, providing users with more accurate and useful search results. Their visionary outlook extended beyond search to include a comprehensive ecosystem of products and services, such as Gmail, Google Maps, and Android, further embedding Google's influence in daily life.

Howard Schultz, the visionary behind Starbucks, revolutionized the coffee industry by transforming coffee consumption into a social and cultural experience. His idea of a "third place" between home and work (where people could relax, connect, and enjoy premium drinks) was initially met with skepticism from investors and industry experts. Many doubted that consumers would pay more for coffee in a café-style environment. Yet Schultz persisted, confident in his belief that Starbucks could offer more than just coffee. His focus on customer experience, employee engagement, and community created a brand that stood apart and grew into a global phenomenon. Today, however, with recent earnings falling short, Starbucks faces new challenges. To stay ahead, it must reconnect with the values that made it special in the first place. Brand leadership, once achieved, must be actively sustained. More often than not, leading brands falter not just because of competitors or shifting tastes, but because of neglecting the core drivers of their success.

Leverage External Expertise

Coming together is a beginning, staying together is progress, and working together is success.

—Henry Ford

Collaborating with external partners can provide valuable expertise and resources. For example, the Swatch team received crucial support from Lego to perfect the quality of the plastic used in their watches. This collaboration was instrumental in overcoming a major production hurdle. Businesses should not hesitate to seek external partnerships when internal resources are insufficient.

Working jointly with other companies or experts can provide access to specialized knowledge, technologies, networks and skills, facilitating innovation and problem-solving. Managers should be open to forming strategic alliances that can enhance their capabilities and accelerate progress. This can be essential for entrepreneurship and innovation. Collaboration facilitates sharing risks and costs associated with innovation projects, enabling firms to explore new opportunities and scale initiatives more effectively.

However, the potential drawbacks of external collaboration also require careful navigation. One challenge is selecting partners aligned with the firm's strategic goals, values, and capabilities to ensure a mutually beneficial relationship. Poorly managed collaborative ventures can lead to conflicts, misaligned objectives, and issues regarding intellectual property rights and knowledge-sharing. Moreover, the openness required for collaboration may expose firms to the risk of knowledge spillovers and imitation by partners, necessitating appropriability strategies to safeguard proprietary information.

To optimize benefits of collaboration, managers can adopt best practices in partnership management. First, clearly defining objectives, roles, and expectations of each partner at the collaboration's outset ensures alignment and transparency. Effective communication channels and conflict resolution mechanisms maintain trust and foster productive relationships.

Building a culture of openness, mutual respect, and continuous learning enhances creativity, innovation, and knowledge-sharing among partners. Regular monitoring, evaluation, and feedback mechanisms track progress, identify areas for improvement, and ensure mutually beneficial and sustainable collaboration.

The early stages of the Swatch story remind us that collaborating with external partners can be vital for driving innovation, enhancing competitiveness, and accelerating growth in businesses. By leveraging diverse expertise and resources while effectively managing challenges, firms can unlock new opportunities, enhance creativity, and achieve sustainable success in the dynamic landscape of entrepreneurship and innovation. The business world is ripe with examples of helpful collaborations particularly in the early stages of a business venture.

In its infancy, Airbnb collaborated with Y Combinator, a startup accelerator, to refine its business model, thus gaining access to mentorship, funding, and networking opportunities. Through this collaboration, Airbnb received invaluable guidance on product development, marketing strategies, and scaling operations, which played a crucial role in its growth from a small startup to a global hospitality platform.

At the outset of Tesla's electric vehicle production, the company collaborated with Panasonic to manufacture lithium-ion batteries for its cars. This collaboration was crucial for Tesla as it enabled the company to access Panasonic's expertise in battery technology and production, ensuring that Tesla's EVs had reliable and high-performance batteries. The partnership between Tesla and Panasonic has since expanded to include joint development of battery technology for energy storage solutions.

Aim for Product–Market Fit

The only way to scale is to first do things that don't scale.

—Reid Hoffman

The quote above highlights the importance of the initial stages of any venture, where focused, hands-on efforts are critical before scaling the business. Before one can reach widespread success, one really needs to put in the hard work of finding what truly resonates with the target market. For example, in the early days of the Swatch project, the team dedicated themselves to understanding the unique desires and preferences of a younger, fashion-conscious audience. They meticulously refined their designs, tested different prototypes, and gathered feedback, all while remaining deeply engaged with their target demographic. This hands-on approach allowed Swatch to develop a product that perfectly aligned with the market's needs, setting the stage for the brand's eventual global success.

Achieving product–market fit (PMF) is a pivotal milestone for any business or startup aiming for sustainable growth. It is the point where a product's value proposition aligns perfectly with the demands of its target market, resulting in widespread acceptance and, ultimately, business success.

A valuable tool for entrepreneurs striving to achieve product–market fit is the PMF cycle framework, prominently developed and popularized by Dan Olsen, a seasoned product management consultant and author. Olsen details this framework in his book *The Lean Product Playbook*, where he outlines a structured, iterative approach to attaining PMF through continuous development, customer feedback, and strategic adaptation. This methodology has become a cornerstone for startups and product teams aiming to systematically identify and sustain PMF.

Let us explore the essential steps of this framework, examining their relevance through the lens of Swatch's success in the 1980s, and discuss how contemporary entrepreneurs can apply these insights to achieve similar outcomes.

1. *Start with a Product Hypothesis and a Big Vision*

   The journey to product–market fit begins with a clear product hypothesis and a compelling vision. This initial step involves defining a value proposition that addresses a specific customer need. For Swatch, the product hypothesis cantered on creating a stylish, affordable watch that would appeal to a younger demographic—a concept that was relatively novel in the watch industry at the time. Swatch envisioned combining Swiss precision with vibrant, playful designs, effectively challenging the traditional perception of Swiss watches as luxury items reserved for the elite.

   However, a successful product hypothesis must be anchored by a bold vision—a broader perspective on how the product can fundamentally change the market. Swatch set out to revolutionize the watch industry by making Swiss-made watches accessible to a much wider audience. They identified an opportunity to disrupt a market that was traditionally dominated by high-end, luxury brands by introducing a product that was innovative not just in design and pricing but also in the way people thought about and purchased watches. Swatch aimed to shift consumer behavior by encouraging customers to buy multiple watches, often mixing and matching them with their outfits, and making watches an object of emotional, often impulsive, buying decisions, something that had been virtually unheard of in the watch industry before.

   For modern entrepreneurs, Swatch's story highlights the importance of formulating a product hypothesis that is deeply rooted in customer insights and coupled with a bold vision for market disruption. This stage is not just about envisioning a product; it's about imagining how that product can transform a market and create new consumer behavior patterns.

2. *Identify a Minimum Viable Segment That Can Be Scaled*

   Once a strong product hypothesis is established, the next critical step is to identify a Minimum Viable Segment (MVS) to test the product. This focused approach ensures that feedback is precise and resources are used efficiently. Swatch identified its MVS as young, fashion-conscious individuals who viewed watches as more than just timekeeping devices but as fashion statements. By targeting this specific segment, Swatch was able to tailor its marketing and product features to meet the unique tastes and preferences of this audience, increasing the likelihood of resonating with them.

Crucially, the MVS should be backed by a market with significant growth potential to support future scaling. Swatch's targeted demographic (youthful consumers who sought stylish and affordable accessories) represented a largely untapped market within the watch industry. This segment provided a solid foundation for the brand's future expansion, allowing Swatch to scale rapidly once the product gained traction.

Entrepreneurs can learn from Swatch's strategic approach by identifying and focusing on a niche market segment with the potential for significant growth. This strategy not only optimizes resource allocation during the early stages but also sets the stage for broader market penetration.

3. *Build a Minimum Viable Business Model*
   Before launching a product, it is essential to develop a minimum viable business model that encompasses a clear positioning strategy, a minimum viable product (MVP), and a go-to-market strategy. Swatch's positioning was unique in that it combined Swiss craftsmanship with affordability and innovative design, a combination that was virtually unheard of at the time. Their MVP was a basic version of their watch that encapsulated the core value proposition—Swiss-made quality in a fashionable, affordable package.

   The go-to-market strategy for Swatch was equally innovative. It included bold marketing campaigns, collaborations with influential designers, and unconventional advertising tactics that emphasized the brand's fresh, youthful image. This strategic approach was instrumental in differentiating Swatch from its competitors and capturing the attention of its target audience.

   For entrepreneurs, building a minimum viable business model involves more than just creating a product. It requires strategically positioning that product in the market, ensuring it resonates with the target audience, and developing a clear, actionable plan for market entry.

4. *Test and Measure Thoroughly*

Thorough testing is a crucial phase in the pursuit of PMF. It involves conducting both quantitative and qualitative assessments to gather data on user behavior and product performance. Swatch encountered several technical challenges during the development of its watches, but these were addressed through relentless testing and refinement. For example, Swatch collaborated with Lego to improve the quality of the plastic used in their watches, a move that exemplified their commitment to quality and innovation.

These rigorous tests provided Swatch with invaluable feedback, allowing the company to fine-tune its product features and ensure that they met customer expectations. The testing phase also involved iterative improvements based on feedback from early users, internal stakeholders, and partners, helping Swatch overcome production hurdles and refine its product to better meet market demands.

Entrepreneurs should view the testing phase as an opportunity to validate assumptions, refine the product, and ensure that it truly aligns with the needs of their target market. This iterative process is where PMF begins to materialize.

5. *Learn and Iterate*

Achieving PMF is not a linear process; it requires continuous learning and iteration. Managers must analyze test results to identify areas for improvement and then make necessary adjustments to the product, positioning, or go-to-market strategy based on the insights gained. Swatch's iterative process involved constant feedback loops from user testing and market reactions, leading to enhancements in design, functionality, and marketing approaches. These adjustments progressively aligned the product closer to market needs and preferences.

Swatch's iterative approach enabled the business to remain agile, allowing it to make necessary adjustments that aligned with evolving consumer preferences. This flexibility was crucial in maintaining the brand's competitive edge and ensuring its sustained appeal.

Entrepreneurs must be prepared to pivot and adapt as new information emerges. The key is to remain flexible, learn from feedback, and iterate until the product is perfectly aligned with market demands.

6. *Scale and Market Penetration*

Once PMF is achieved, the focus shifts to scaling and market penetration. Swatch's extensive and bold marketing campaigns, innovative product designs, and strategic market positioning enabled the brand to capture a significant share of the market. Swatch's unique identity and widespread appeal were instrumental in its successful market penetration, transforming it from a disruptive newcomer into a global phenomenon.

Swatch's scaling strategy involved aggressive marketing and the expansion of its distribution networks globally. The brand's ability to maintain a consistent image while scaling was key to its widespread acceptance and success.

For entrepreneurs, the scaling phase represents an opportunity to amplify their success. It's crucial to ensure that the product not only maintains its market fit but also expands its reach and impact as it scales.

7. *Sustain Product–Market Fit*

Maintaining PMF is an ongoing challenge that requires continuous adaptation and innovation. The market landscape is dynamic, with consumer preferences and competitive pressures constantly evolving. Swatch's ability to continually introduce fresh designs and stay ahead of fashion trends was critical to its sustained relevance and success in a highly competitive market. This adaptability is essential for long-term success and continued market fit.

Entrepreneurs must recognize that achieving PMF is not a one-time event but an ongoing process. Sustaining market fit requires a commitment to continuous innovation and a keen awareness of market shifts. The ability to anticipate and respond to changes in the market is crucial for maintaining a competitive edge.

In conclusion, the story of Swatch is a good example of how achieving and sustaining PMF can lead to market success. By applying the PMF cycle framework, entrepreneurs can navigate the complex journey from product hypothesis to market leadership. Swatch's success can serve as a blueprint for modern entrepreneurs, demonstrating the importance of starting with a strong product hypothesis, focusing on a scalable market segment, building a viable business model, and continuously testing, learning, and iterating.

Ultimately, the key to achieving PMF lies in understanding and responding to customer needs, being willing to adapt and innovate, and maintaining a clear vision for the future. By following these principles, entrepreneurs can create products that not only fit the market but also redefine it.

Build a Brand, Not Just a Product

Products are made in the factory, but brands are created in the mind.
—Walter Landor

Imagine walking through a bustling market where you stumble upon a vendor selling counterfeit luxury watches. These fakes are sometimes crafted with such precision that they are often virtually indistinguishable from the real thing. Some of them are built by reverse-engineering the genuine item to its smallest detail; they may contain a movement that is an almost exact clone of the real thing. Even an expert collector would struggle to tell the fake from the genuine item. Yet, despite their identical appearance and operation, buyers are hardly ever willing to pay the same price for something they know to be a replica as they would for the authentic item.

This scenario highlights the profound impact of branding on consumer perception and value. While the counterfeit and genuine products may share the same functional attributes, a true brand offers something far more elusive: an emotional connection, a narrative of heritage or prestige, and a promise of quality and exclusivity.

A brand carries a storied legacy that cannot be replicated by only physical attributes. It is often this intangible and psychological allure that justifies the premium price of the authentic product. Consumers are investing in the brand's reputation, history, and unique experience it offers, which a counterfeit simply cannot provide. This stark difference in perceived value underscores how a brand's essence transcends its physical manifestation, creating a powerful differentiation that product features alone cannot achieve.

A brand allows you to elevate a product beyond its tangible features and design, creating a powerful source of differentiation. As a tangible asset that cannot be easily replicated, a brand can be a critical source of sustainable competitive advantage. It can create enormous value for both the customers who buy and the companies that nurture them.

For customers, brands act as important signaling devices. Not only do they help identify the source of a product, but they also function as a promise, bond, or pact between the customer and the company. They set expectations and can carry a lot of symbolic (as well as functional) meaning, which can help minimize uncertainty, purchase risks, and search cost. Brands can help speed up decision making, aid us in taking more informed decisions, and generally make our lives easier.

For organizations, strong brands confer differentiation, competitive advantages, and legal protection; they can also significantly contribute to financial value. Consider, for example, a brand like Coca-Cola. In 2023, its market capitalization was about $270 billion. That same year, Interbrand (the global brand consultancy firm that has become a leader in brand valuation) estimated that the Coca-Cola brand alone was worth approximately $58 billion. This suggests that a significant portion of Coca-Cola's market value (more than 20 percent) is attributed to the brand alone, highlighting the immense financial impact of Coca-Cola's brand equity. It is unlikely that any other single asset owned by the Coca-Cola company accounts for such a high percentage of its market capitalization.

A brand generates financial value for a company through several key mechanisms. First, it can influence people's hearts and minds. In other words, it can make us think or feel in a certain way, which in turn influences our behavior.

From an emotional standpoint, the Swatch brand evoked a sense of fun and creativity, while also appealing to our rational side, through a promise of reliability and high quality. This connection of the emotional with the rational encouraged customers to choose Swatch over other brands, engendering loyalty, repeat purchases, and a willingness to pay a higher price than for generic watches. So, by shaping consumer perceptions and behaviors, Swatch could improve its cash flow and generate real financial value, not just customer value.

What is a good cash flow, and how does marketing and branding improve it? In general, to create financial value, a business should aim to improve four aspects of its cash flow: the level, the speed, the duration, and the risk profile of cash flow. Using Swatch as an example, let's see how a strong brand can help achieve these objectives in practice.

First, to improve the level of cash flow, a strong brand can help by driving sales growth and improving operating margins. Swatch was able to drive sales volume by attracting new customers and encouraging repeat purchases. Through a bold, creative, and yet frugal marketing strategy, Swatch was able to consistently draw in both new and returning customers at low cost, improving cash flow levels. As sales volumes rose, Swatch benefited from economies of scale, where unit costs decreased, and operational efficiency improved.

A strong brand can enhance operating margins by enabling higher prices, reducing costs, and achieving economies of scale. Swatch, for example, commanded a premium price within its low-market position, by offering a strong, appealing brand. The buzz around the brand, and its reputation for stylish and accessible watches, meant consumers were willing to pay more, thus improving profit margins. Marketing efforts that encourage word-of-mouth effects can also cut costs associated with expensive advertising. By growing its sales volume, Swatch was able to spread fixed costs over more units, further improving margins.

The power of branding in enhancing profit margins cannot be overstated. For example, many prestigious watch brands incorporate relatively affordable and generic ETA movements into their timepieces. Yet they still manage to command exorbitant prices in the marketplace. For instance, a watch that may cost just a few hundred dollars to manufacture may fetch several thousand dollars when sold.

Georges Kern, the former CEO of IWC Watches, drew some criticism several years ago for a remark he made during a lecture in Zurich. He admitted that the profit margin for a luxury brand like IWC doesn't primarily stem from the watch's features, but rather from the compelling marketing and storytelling that accompany it. This admission sparked some controversy, as it highlighted the significant role of branding and perception in the luxury market, potentially overshadowing the intrinsic quality and craftsmanship of the products themselves.

The substantial difference between production costs and retail price exemplifies the influence of branding. Consumers are not just purchasing a functional timepiece; they are investing in the brand's heritage, craftsmanship, and perceived exclusivity. Many watch brands have meticulously cultivated their identities over decades, becoming synonymous with luxury, precision, and status. This strategic brand positioning allows them to justify premium pricing and achieve higher profit margins than their manufacturing costs alone would suggest. And of course, this may be achieved in any industry, not just luxury. People are willing to pay more for a bottle of Heinz ketchup, a box of Kellogg's Corn Flakes, or a Lindt chocolate tablet than a generic competitor, even though the difference in taste between the alternatives may not be immediately discernible and the production costs may be similar.

What about speed of cash flow, the second aspect of healthy cash flow? Strong brands can accelerate the speed of cash flow by accelerating market penetration and building loyalty. Swatch's dynamic promotional campaigns, its leveraging of influencers and trendsetters, and its adaptive and creative designs meant they were always able to penetrate markets quickly. Its ability to create a buzz with its marketing strategy and a strong related emotional connection with customers ensured people were more likely to buy new products upon release (often multiple purchases), providing a quicker revenue stream.

Third, brands can also help extend the duration of cash flow, for example, by providing organizations with a sustainable and defendable source of competitive advantage. Extending cash flow duration means ensuring long-term market presence. Swatch's strong brand equity is an intangible asset that provides a sustainable competitive advantage, making it difficult for competitors to replicate its success quickly. In addition, continuously identifying new market opportunities extends cash flow duration. Swatch's willingness to explore new product lines, designs, and market segments contributed to a long-lasting cash flow.

Finally, brands also create financial value by reducing the riskiness of cash flow. For example, a brand can help develop strong connections and high customer satisfaction, which can mitigate business risks. Swatch's commitment to quality and innovative designs ensures a satisfied customer base, reducing the threat from competitors and stabilizing cash flow.

The customer loyalty that often comes with a resonant brand also reduces the need for constant investment in customer acquisition. Swatch's loyal customer base meant lower marketing costs to attract new buyers, resulting in more stable and predictable cash flows. Loyal customers are less likely to switch to competitors, providing a steady revenue stream and reducing financial volatility.

So, by improving these four areas (level, speed, duration, and riskiness of cash flow), a brand can significantly enhance a company's financial performance. Swatch exemplifies how strategic marketing can not only drive immediate sales and profitability but also ensure long-term financial health and resilience against market fluctuations.

Effective brand management, in essence, entails building and sustaining brand equity. Brand equity denotes the differential effect of brand knowledge on consumer responses to marketing. Positive brand equity signifies that consumers react more favorably to branded products than unbranded ones. For example, Apple exemplifies strong positive brand equity. The Apple brand is associated with innovation, quality, and a seamless user experience, leading consumers to willingly pay premium prices for their products and eagerly anticipate new releases. This positive perception enhances Apple's market position and profitability.

Positive brand equity enhances customer trust and loyalty by cementing itself in their hearts and minds. Conversely, negative brand equity occurs when consumers react unfavorably to a brand. One notable example is Juul, a brand in the e-cigarette industry. Despite its initial success, Juul faced significant backlash caused by concerns about its marketing efforts to position as "cool" a product with health risks that could promote underage smoking and be subject to regulatory scrutiny. This negative perception damaged Juul's reputation and led to declining sales as consumers and policymakers alike questioned the brand's ethics and impact on public health.

How can a business establish strong and positive brand equity? In essence, it requires fostering strong, favorable, and unique associations with the brand through resonant experiences. This involves adeptly managing two key components: brand awareness and brand image. High brand awareness facilitates learning and increases the likelihood of consideration during purchase. A positive brand image, developed through consistent messaging, strong associations, and unique positioning, reinforces the brand's allure. Building brand awareness and a positive brand image offers several key benefits, including increased customer loyalty, higher perceived value, and a competitive edge in the market.

Brand awareness makes it easy for customers to learn about the brand. Once it is in memory, customers can begin to build brand associations. Awareness increases the likelihood that the brand will be part of customers' evoked set (i.e., a mental list of brands that are considered for purchase in a certain product category). Also, higher awareness of a brand may lead to choosing that brand over others, even though there are no other associations to that brand. This is particularly true for low involvement purchases, where product choices are based purely on recognition.

To create a positive brand image, companies need to link strong, favorable, and unique associations to the brand. "Strong" means that the brand messages must be consistent, and the brand relevant to customers. "Favorable" means that one needs to position the brand in a way that is desired by customers (i.e., make it positive). "Unique" means giving customers something distinctive and different that can be transformational for customers.

Customers can form brand associations in a variety of ways. For example, they can originate through personal experiences with the brand, through promotion such as advertising, through consumer reports, and through word-of-mouth promotion by other customers, influencers' advice, and by assumption based on the brand name, logo, and other intangibles. So, focusing attention on things like advertising and social media is not the only direct way in which we can build a brand image. The wise marketer will leverage all available avenues. For example, Google does very little advertising, yet it has a near unique and strong brand image by harnessing user-generated experiences.

The success of brands like Zara, Lululemon, Supreme, Tesla and Costco are a reminder that building a strong brand presence doesn't always require significant investment in traditional advertising. By focusing on customer experience, product quality, and the leveraging of organic marketing strategies, they have successfully cultivated strong brand recognition and image.

The two components of brand equity (brand awareness and associations) are a necessary but not sufficient element of brand equity. In other words, you typically need both to build strong brand equity. The success of the Swatch brand is a testament to the simultaneous building of brand awareness and the cultivation of unique, strong, and favorable brand associations.

Swatch strategically established itself in the market by creating a memorable and easily recognizable brand that quickly became part of the customers' evoked set. It created strong associations via consistent and relevant brand messages centered around fun, creativity, and affordability. They were all favorable associations too, which positioned Swatch as a trendy yet accessible option, a desirable characteristic for many consumers. The association proved to be quite unique, as it was the only watch positioned as a fashion accessory that also told the time.

Initially, Swatch faced many of the challenges common to any startup in brand development, such as limited resources, difficulties in standing out in a competitive market dominated by established brands, communicating a unique value proposition and distinct brand identity, earning consumer trust and credibility without an established reputation, maintaining consistent messaging across all channels with a small team, and so on. Addressing these challenges requires strategic planning, resourcefulness, creative problem-solving, and a focus on delivering consistent and compelling brand experiences to build a strong and lasting brand identity.

The concept of Minimum Viable Brand (MVB) is a useful strategic approach for startups to develop a brand identity that resonates with target audiences while conserving resources. The MVB framework emphasizes the creation of a foundational brand identity that captures the startup's value proposition and connects with the desired market segment.

By focusing on essential brand elements (such as brand purpose, values, and visual identity) startups can establish strong brand recognition and credibility without overinvesting in elaborate branding initiatives. This iterative approach allows startups to test and refine their brand positioning, messaging, and perceivable identity based on market feedback, ensuring alignment with customer preferences and market trends.

The key elements of a MVB for a startup should generally include the following:

- *Brand Purpose*: To clearly define the company's mission and the core reason it exists, which resonates with the target audience. For example, Swatch aimed to democratize high-quality watches by making them fun, affordable, and accessible to a broad audience, chiming with consumers seeking both style and affordability.
- *Brand Values*: To establish fundamental beliefs and principles that guide the company's actions and decision-making processes. Swatch embraced values of innovation, creativity, and accessibility, guiding their product development and marketing strategies.
- *Visual Identity*: To develop a cohesive visual identity, including a logo, color scheme, and typography, that represents the brand's essence and appeals to the target market. Swatch created a distinctive visual identity with bold, colorful designs and a recognizable logo, making their watches instantly identifiable and appealing.
- *Brand Positioning*: To articulate a unique value proposition and positioning statement that differentiates the brand from competitors. Swatch positioned itself as a fashion accessory telling the time, setting itself apart through its playful and innovative designs.
- *Messaging*: To craft clear and consistent messaging that communicates the brand's purpose, values, and benefits to its audience. Swatch's messaging consistently highlighted the fun, creative, and accessible nature of their products, reinforcing their brand purpose and values in every communication.
- *Iterative Testing*: To continuously examine and refine brand elements based on market feedback and customer insights to ensure alignment with customer preferences and buying trends. Swatch regularly introduced new designs, limited editions, and other marketing assets using customer feedback to refine their offerings and stay in tune with market trends.
- *Agile Adaptation*: To adopt a flexible approach to branding, allowing for rapid adjustments and improvements in response to

market dynamics and customer needs. Swatch's ability to adapt swiftly to changing fashion trends and consumer preferences helped them maintain relevance and appeal in the dynamic watch market.

By focusing on these key elements, companies like Swatch that face challenges typical of any startup can begin to build a compelling brand presence that drives customer engagement, loyalty, and eventually long-term success.

Sources and Further Readings

Aaker, D. A. 1996. *Building Strong Brands*. Free Press.

Ahuja, G. 2000. "Collaboration Networks, Structural Holes, and Innovation: A Longitudinal Study." *Administrative Science Quarterly* 45 (3): 425–455.

Chesbrough, H., W. Vanhaverbeke, and J. West. 2006. *Open Innovation: Researching a New Paradigm*. Oxford University Press.

Day, G. S. 1990. *Market-Driven Strategy: Processes for Creating Value*. Free Press.

Doyle, P. 2000. *Value-Based Marketing: Marketing Strategies for Corporate Growth and Shareholder Value*. Wiley.

Gardner, J. 2014. *The Entrepreneur's Guide to the Lean Brand: How to Create a Powerful Brand with Limited Resources*. Market by Numbers.

Hamel, G., and C. K. Prahalad. 1994. *Competing for the Future*. Harvard Business School Press.

Kapferer, J.-N. 2012. *The New Strategic Brand Management: Advanced Insights and Strategic Thinking*. 5th ed. Kogan Page.

Keller, K. L. 1993. "Conceptualizing, Measuring, and Managing Customer-Based Brand Equity." *Journal of Marketing* 57 (1): 1–22.

Keller, K. L. 2003. "Brand Synthesis: The Multidimensionality of Brand Knowledge." *Journal of Consumer Research* 29 (4): 595–600.

Keller, K. L. 2013. *Strategic Brand Management: Building, Measuring, and Managing Brand Equity*. 4th ed. Pearson.

Keller, K. L., and D. R. Lehmann. 2006. "Brands and Branding: Research Findings and Future Priorities." *Marketing Science* 25 (6): 740–759.

Lukas, B. A., G. J. Whitwell, and P. Doyle. 2003. "How Can a Shareholder Value Approach Improve Marketing's Strategic Influence?" *Journal of Business Research* 56 (3): 203–210.

Miller, D., and P. H. Friesen. 1980. Momentum and Revolution in Organizational Adaptation." *Academy of Management Journal* 23 (4): 591–614.

Nambisan, S. 2002. "Designing Virtual Customer Environments for New Product Development: Toward a Theory." *Academy of Management Review* 27 (3): 392–413.

Noble, C. H., and M. P. Mokwa. 1999. "Implementing Marketing Strategies: Developing and Testing a Managerial Theory." *Journal of Marketing* 63 (4): 57–73.

Olsen, D. 2015. *The Lean Product Playbook: How to Innovate with Minimum Viable Products and Rapid Customer Feedback.* Wiley.

Park, C. W., D. J. McInnis, and A. B. Eisingerich. 2016. *Brand Admiration: Building a Business People Love.* Routledge.

Rothaermel, F. T. 2015. *Strategic Management: Concepts and Cases.* 3rd ed. McGraw-Hill Education.

Smith, P. G., and D. G. Reinertsen. 1985. *Strategic Flexibility: A Management Guide for Changing Times.* Van Nostrand Reinhold.

Walter, S., F. Heinemann, P. Haberstock, and T. Wiesmann. 2023. "Building a Minimum Viable Brand—Best Practice for Startups." *Marketing Review St.Gallen* 40 (3): 62–69.

Yohn, D. L. 2014. "Startups Need a Minimum Viable Brand" *Harvard Business Review*, June 13. https://hbr.org/2014/06/start-ups-need-a-minimum-viable-brand

CHAPTER 5

The Marketing Team

The initial Swatch marketing team was a small but mighty duo, consisting of just Theile and his personal assistant, Mrs. Emilia Balasso.

Konstantin Theile was born in 1951 in Chile, the child of Albert and Gerda Theile, renowned writers and journalists. His twin sister, Johanna Maria, is a distinguished academic at the University of Chile. At the age of two, Theile relocated to Switzerland, and later lived in Spain, Italy, and Germany, where he attended boarding school. As a result of these frequent moves, he attended a total of 12 different schools. In 1970, he studied French at l'université de Grenoble, before enrolling in a Hotel Training School in Glion sur Montreux.

However, his first job at a Mövenpick Restaurant made him realize that this was not his true calling. As a result, in 1973, he decided to study economics at the University of St. Gallen, followed by a doctoral degree, from which he graduated in 1981. During this time, he also studied sociology at the University of Konstanz, a subject that deeply fascinated him.

In parallel, Theile joined a graduate program at UBS. Then, in 1980, he joined the pharmaceutical division of F. Hoffman-La Roche & Co. AG in Basel, taking charge of the Polish, Yugoslavian, and Albanian offices. This job offered him an up-close encounter with the realities of living under a communist regime. While his initial ambition was to lead the pharmaceutical division of a foreign subsidiary, such as Indonesia, he was disappointed to learn that this would take at least 5 years. His impatience to reach a senior position quickly led him to join ETA SA in Grenchen in 1982.

Theile's values and career aspirations were clearly shaped by an exposure to various cultures, industries, and social concerns, leading him to seek roles to effect meaningful change. These early experiences helped him develop an ability to adjust and made him inquisitive and very determined; it also conferred him with the capacity to embrace and learn from unfamiliar situations.

Theile was blessed to have a highly competent and reliable partner in Mrs. Balasso. She was an absolute powerhouse at ETA, known for her efficiency and deep institutional knowledge. With years of experience under her belt, she was the backbone of the marketing team—a vital cog in the very well-oiled machine that was ETA.

Mrs. Balasso's knowledge of the company was unparalleled. She knew every employee by name, their role within the organization, and their whereabouts at any given moment. She navigated the labyrinthine bureaucracy of 1980s Swiss corporate culture with the dexterity of a seasoned professional. Whether it was negotiations, facilitation, or coordination, she conducted them all with grace and finesse. Even as the team continued to grow, she remained the undisputed expert in all things ETA. Her understanding of the company's operations and intricate workings was unmatched. It would be very safe indeed to say that Mrs. Balasso was an invaluable asset to the team.

Another member from the very beginning was Eddy Scheidegger, who joined the team a few weeks before the market launch in Switzerland. He was the "logistician" who had the very challenging task of matching sales and production.

Theile and his team were the driving force behind the global marketing launch of the Swatch, reporting directly to Thomke and, a few months later, to Jacques Irniger, the Marketing Director of ETA. Irniger, a seasoned marketing executive with experience at Colgate-Palmolive and Nestlé, had been handpicked by Thomke in 1983 to bring more expertise in mass marketing to the whole company.

Marketing consultant Sprecher also remained involved for a while as an external consultant, adding more depth to the team, particularly when it came to Swatch's advertising efforts and its relationship with the advertising agency McCann Erickson. He provided occasional support until the summer of 1983. Sprecher's last major contribution was to support the launch of Swatch in the American market. His legacy of being a crucial figure in the initial shaping and triumph of the Swatch concept would forever live on.

As Swatch's ambitions grew and expanded into uncharted territories in early 1983, so did its team. The once modest unit started to blossom into a larger force, determined to conquer new markets and establish their dominance. The first market to fall quickly under their spell was their home country of Switzerland.

Why did the Swiss market embrace Swatch so readily? Perhaps it was the growing concern over the decline of their esteemed watch industry. Faced with the threat of obsolescence, the Swiss watch sector needed a revival, and Swatch provided a compelling solution. With a simple yet powerful message—by purchasing a Swatch, consumers could help safeguard their country's watchmaking heritage—the brand struck a chord with national pride. This strategic positioning not only reassured Swiss consumers but also transformed Swatch into a symbol of resilience, ensuring its strong foothold in the domestic market.

With one market conquered, the team then set their sights on the UK, France, Germany, and the United States. These markets required a different approach than the one adopted for the Swiss market, necessitating the addition of skilled salesmen who could navigate the unique landscapes and spend significant time there.

The UK was quickly dealt with by collaborating with a local partner who offered to purchase and sell a large quantity of Swatches himself. He demonstrated success in these efforts.

Expanding into the French, German, and U.S. markets, on the other hand, demanded the expansion of Swatch's marketing team by hiring country managers within the team in Switzerland. This strategic move was crucial for establishing a strong presence and driving sales in these countries.

Enter Roger Guyard, known by everyone simply as "the Frenchman"—a mysterious individual, with a commanding presence and an unquenchable thirst for success. Even as a newcomer to the watch industry, the Frenchman exuded a certain allure that ensnared the entire marketing team at Swatch. With a background in the military, he possessed impeccable organizational skills, a sharp intellect, and a logical mind that worked at lightning speed. He had boldly approached the Swatch marketing team with a job application shortly after the Zurich press conference, and from the moment he met Theile, there was an undeniable chemistry.

Theile, a strong advocate for intuition and the "power of gut feeling," knew that once his instincts were triggered, they were worth taking seriously. He firmly believed that decisions should be first evaluated based on instinct and feelings and only then should logic and rationality come into play. For him, the heart always led the mind. To ignore this principle was to risk missing out on valuable opportunities. This philosophy had guided Theile throughout his life, making him open to new ideas and willing to take bold risks.

Although the Frenchman passed Theile's gut-feeling test, his demands for a high salary were a major problem. The Swatch team just couldn't afford him. As a result, Theile politely and regrettably rejected his job application, feeling guilty for possibly passing up on a talented individual. Yet the Frenchman was not one to back down easily. He proposed a deal: to build up the French market within a month, without a salary, only requesting that his expenses be reimbursed. Then, upon achievement of his projected expansion, he could stay on with pay. Despite Swatch already struggling with its budget, Theile was intrigued and accepted the challenge, fully aware that taking on this risk could potentially jeopardize the entire project.

The Frenchman's unconventional approach proved successful, quickly generating interest and increasing sales in the French market. Over the years, Theile and the Frenchman became close friends. Their collaboration on the Swatch project forged a strong professional relationship.

The Frenchman was brimming with innovative ideas. His first move was to enlist the expertise of a prestigious PR agency in France, led by one of the country's most creative minds. Together with the PR team, he launched a wildly successful and imaginative marketing campaign that seamlessly aligned with Swatch's brand positioning.

With limited financial resources, Swatch had to be resourceful in maximizing brand exposure without breaking the bank. This called for clever thinking, and the French PR team certainly delivered. For example, instead of investing in a costly full-page newspaper advert, they proposed a clever alternative: five smaller ads strategically placed in the corners of a page. Not only did this save Swatch a significant amount of money, but it also made the ads stand out in a unique and attention-grabbing way.

Another idea from the Frenchman and the PR team centered on the power of storytelling. Recognizing Swatch as a visionary brand, they understood the importance of storytelling from the outset. The inventive

French team took this concept further by crafting captivating short stories published in a local newspaper, drawing readers in like a soap opera and creating a magnetic appeal around the brand. These stories, revolving around fashion, were a weekly feature that started to capture the hearts and minds of thousands of readers. The Swatch brand was seamlessly interwoven into these captivating tales, not necessarily as a focal element of the story, but as a strategically placed accessory that elevated the story to new heights.

The characters were crafted with depth and complexity, making them more intriguing than they might otherwise have been. The storytelling evoked strong emotions, leaving readers on the edge of their seats. The resonant voice used in the stories was rich with character, further immersing readers into the world of Swatch. This novel approach to product placement not only boosted the brand's visibility but also created a loyal following of readers who eagerly awaited each new installment and who would go on to become enthusiastic consumers. Swatch proved that storytelling is a powerful tool that can effectively showcase a brand without being overtly commercial.

Another propitious and innovative idea was to launch the Swatch watch in France not at a watch fair, but at the Paris Prêt-à-Porter fashion show, with the marketing slogan "a fashion accessory showing time" being very apt indeed. Not only would this help Swatch position itself as a fashion accessory, but the worldwide fashion press would be present too, so their interest in the Swatch could be piqued.

Suddenly, Swatch was no longer just a watch but also a coveted fashion accessory speaking volumes about one's personal style. The team was able to masterfully position Swatch as a must-have fashion statement.

This clever positioning did not go unnoticed. One day, the head designer of Van Cleef & Arpels in Paris came up with the idea of designing a joint Swatch. Theile and the Frenchman met several times at Place Vendôme in Paris to discuss the idea. Unfortunately, it was estimated that the joint watch project would have cost several thousand Swiss francs, well beyond Swatch's budget. So, alas, financial prudence meant that this plan was abandoned. Who knows what the result of this collaboration would have led to, and the opportunity that might have been missed?

After the Frenchman, the fourth full-time employee to join the Swatch marketing team was a young Swiss man called Christoph Keigel, tasked with conquering the German market. Fresh out of university and lacking formal work experience, his passion and hunger for knowledge meant he was a valuable person to have on board.

Keigel's deep understanding of the target market set him truly apart. He was like a chameleon, seamlessly blending into the culture and speaking the language of the target market. His youthful energy and innovative ideas breathed new life into the team, making him an integral part of Swatch's German market success. Keigel was a true representation of the Swatch brand: bold, dynamic, and always on the cutting edge.

Finally, another pivotal team member was the extravagant Max Imgrüth, joining Swatch's ranks from his office in New York. Known affectionately as "Mad Max," he played a crucial role in Swatch's triumph in the United States. Max possessed an exceptional intuition for the types of designs that would captivate American consumers. His keen sense of trends and awareness of evolving styles ensured that Swatch consistently hit the mark in the competitive U.S. market. Max's contributions were instrumental in shaping the brand's U.S. image thus securing its widespread popularity.

The core Swiss team comprising Theile, Irniger, Sprecher, and often also Thomke, worked tirelessly, putting in long hours and late nights, fuelled by their passion and determination. Despite lacking experience in the watch industry (or perhaps because of it) they became a tightly knit group, constantly discussing and exchanging their innovative ideas and experiences. Pizza and beer were often their dinner of choice as they gathered till late in the office, brainstorming and strategizing for upcoming Swatch campaigns.

Their dedication was evident in the countless hours they spent analyzing market activities and refining proposals for advertising and public relations agencies. The small size of their team enabled a hands-on approach, fostering an environment where everyone gained valuable experience. The office buzzed with energy as the quartet threw themselves into their work, each member contributing their unique perspectives and strengths, creating a dynamic and collaborative atmosphere.

Generating radical ideas was crucial to the triumph of the small Swatch marketing team. Their naivety, while risky, often paid off in spades. With limited resources and a tight budget, they were forced into frugal innovation, tapping into their creativity and executing ideas with only a fraction of funds available than might otherwise might have been the case.

Without the luxury of a bottomless budget, even the thought of spending a few hundred francs would make them break out in a sweat. This financial constraint forced them to accomplish what many brands would with five-digit sums, using only three. Their ingenuity became the driving force behind cost-effective yet highly impactful projects, delivering impressive returns on investment and propelling sales to new heights.

Swatch achieved a monumental triumph in its early days despite being led by individuals with no prior experience in the watch industry. This extraordinary feat was made possible by a handful of crucial factors.

Perhaps the most pivotal element was the team's unwavering focus on creating not just another watch but, instead, a fashion accessory. The team defied convention, because they were not entrenched in the watch industry's traditional ways of thinking. Their lack of expertise and their naivety were, in fact, one of their greatest strengths. This allowed them to think outside the box, unfettered by the constraints of industry norms. Had the team consisted of individuals from the watch industry, this bold and daring approach would not have been contemplated, resulting in yet just another timepiece. Theile's team consistently turned down offers of help from watch industry experts and consultants, not only due to a lack of funds but also to avoid relying only on the same old strategies.

In addition, the team was highly effective due to their agility, diversity, and youthful energy. They had an uncanny ability to empathize with their customers, intuitively understanding their deepest desires and translating those insights into products that genuinely resonated. Importantly, as members of the target market themselves, they brought firsthand insight, which proved invaluable in shaping products that truly connected with their audience.

They were also not afraid to take risks and to experiment and learn from their own experiences as well as from their customers. And when mistakes were made, as they inevitably were, they embraced them and used them as stepping stones toward greater success. Thomke had once passionately declared to Theile, his voice booming with conviction:

"Mistakes are necessary! If you don't make them, it's a clear sign that you're not taking risks. But if you foolishly repeat the same mistake, it's a blatant sign of your stupidity!"

So as Swatch embarked on its ambitious journey to take charge of the global watch market, the initial marketing team, led by Theile, and supported by the indispensable Mrs. Balasso, laid the groundwork for the brand's meteoric rise. Together, they navigated the complexities of launching Swatch in Switzerland, reassuring the nation it would not lose its revered watch industry by igniting national pride and enthusiasm. Their success in Switzerland paved the way for expansion into key markets like the UK, France, Germany, and the United States, where innovative local marketing strategies were employed to establish Swatch as a coveted fashion accessory.

The addition of key team members like Roger Guyard, the enigmatic Frenchman, the youthful and dynamic Christoph Keigel, and the insightful and flamboyant Max Imgrüth—or Mad Max—injected fresh energy and ideas into the group, propelling Swatch to new heights. Despite their lack of experience in the watch industry, the team's agility, diversity, and willingness to take risks proved to be their greatest assets. And as Swatch continued to defy conventions and push the limits of originality, the foundation was laid for unconventional product and clever positioning strategies, centered on a marketing mix that had never been witnessed before in the watch industry.

Commentary and Managerial Insights

Surround Yourself with the Right People

We rise by lifting others.

—Robert Ingersoll

Luck becomes more attainable when surrounded by the right people. Clearly, Swatch's revolutionary product and process innovation could not have been achieved without the exceptional leadership of Thomke. His visionary guidance and unswerving determination were the driving forces behind this groundbreaking success.

Thomke combined his entrepreneurial spirit and science and engineering skills with the instinct of recruiting the right people. He had the courage of the outsider to take on the conservative structure prevailing within a large corporation at the time. His vision, leadership, and willingness to take risks were instrumental in the creation and success of the Swatch. His contributions to the watchmaking industry earned him recognition as one of the most influential figures in horology.

Thomke might have been the visionary leader, but without the collaborative brilliance of Elmar Mock and Jacques Müller, the Swatch watch would just have remained an unfulfilled dream. Their collective ingenuity ignited the initial spark that gave birth to the Swatch. The combined talents and insights of these three individuals would shape the watch industry's landscape forever. Their collaboration highlights the power of teamwork in driving innovation, showing that success often emerges from the synergy of multiple minds working toward a common goal. And when Theile and his entire sub-team combined their efforts with a clever marketing strategy, Swatch quickly became a global phenomenon.

The Swatch marketing team, though initially small, incubated a powerhouse of creativity, determination, and adaptability. They exemplify the importance of diversity and agility in problem-solving. Their backgrounds spanned various industries and cultures, providing them with a rich tapestry of perspectives to draw from. But curiously (and perhaps crucially, as we have shared in relation to local market teams), they also had very little experience in the watch industry.

Their diversity and "outsider perspective" fuelled their ability to innovate and think outside the box, enabling them to devise groundbreaking marketing strategies that defied industry norms. Moreover, a willingness to take risks and embrace failure as part of the learning process was vital. The leadership team understood that mistakes were not only inevitable but even essential for growth. By daring to experiment and iterate, they were able to refine their approach to deliver remarkable results.

Additionally, the Swatch team's relentless focus on creating not just a product but in reality a cultural phenomenon underscores the importance of understanding and connecting with customers on a deeper psychological level. They tapped into the emotions and aspirations of their target audience, positioning Swatch as more than a cheap plastic watch but rather a symbol of personal expression and style.

The success of Swatch's leadership and marketing teams is also a reminder that formal training and industry experience may not always be required, especially when dealing with radical innovation. Theile didn't have much of a background in marketing, and his experience in the watch industry was almost nonexistent. He was surrounded by an equally inexperienced team who, like him, were willing and able to learn. This highlights the importance of passion and learning by doing. Theile's team possessed zeal, an inherent desire to learn new things; they remained intuitive and confident enough to make calculated decisions based on gut feeling.

This serves as a reminder that the size of a team matters far less than the motivation and drive of its members. The Swatch marketing squad, though consisting of only five people in its first 2 years, managed to sell around 3 million watches in a single year by 1984. Their success underscores that it's not about the number of team members but their attitude and commitment. These few motivated and youthful individuals thrived on experimentation, learning from their experiences, and embracing their mistakes as opportunities for growth.

They successfully secured Swatch products in major department stores, positioned the brand as a fashion accessory that also happened to show the time, and convinced the Swiss market to embrace these plastic watches. The youthful nature of the team, mirroring many of the characteristics of their target market, fostered natural empathy and deep brand affinity.

Additionally, Theile—much like Thomke—believed in empowering his team members by granting them significant autonomy and influence over key decisions. Managing people within a business, in his view, is akin to conducting an orchestra. If you can clearly envision and communicate the kind of sound you want to create, and you surround yourself with talented musicians who are passionate about their craft, all that's left is to give them the freedom and latitude to play the music in their own creative and original styles.

The success of Swatch was not solely attributed to its managers and engineers; a critical contribution also came from the skilled workers responsible for handcrafting the watches in its initial phase. Recognizing the pivotal role of these assembly workers, the Swatch marketing and engineering team actively engaged with them to ensure their satisfaction by soliciting their valuable input in the production process.

These workers proved a linchpin in advising the company on the necessary machinery upgrades to facilitate production scalability. From an initial output of a few hundred watches per day in the first weeks, Swatch rapidly expanded its manufacturing capacity to 2.5 million units by 1984. At the zenith of its success, Swatch achieved an annual sales volume of 30 million units, underscoring the indispensable contribution of its assembly workforce to its remarkable growth trajectory.

Creating agile teams and tapping into diverse backgrounds and experiences can also fuel innovation and success. The initial Swatch marketing unit, with its small size and varied perspectives, swiftly generated and executed ideas, paradoxically benefiting from their lack of prior industry experience. Cultivating a startup-like environment within teams fosters agility and innovation, empowering every member to contribute ideas and take ownership for dynamic and effective strategies. Embracing mistakes as learning opportunities, as emphasized by Thomke, is critical for growth, encouraging risk-taking and continuous improvement.

Building a cohesive and motivated team—like the close-knit Swatch marketing group—drives success through shared passion, collaboration, and recognition of individual contributions, underscoring the need for business leaders to prioritize these elements to boost performance and innovation. Building such a team involves fostering a culture of excellence, mutual trust, and shared purpose, where each member is empowered to contribute their best to collective success.

By prioritizing the recruitment, development, and retention of top talent, organizations can build a strong foundation for sustainable growth, innovation, and competitive advantage. Numerous successful companies have exemplified these principles, by assembling high-performing teams that drive organizational success.

Pixar Animation Studios, under the leadership of Ed Catmull and Steve Jobs, prioritized hiring exceptionally talented individuals who shared a passion for storytelling and creativity. This focus on assembling a team of top animators, writers, and directors with diverse backgrounds and perspectives contributed to Pixar's string of blockbuster hits to cement its reputation as an industry leader in animated filmmaking.

Similarly, Google, founded by Larry Page and Sergey Brin, built its success on hiring brilliant engineers to foster a culture of innovation and collaboration. By assembling a team of top technical talent and then aligning them with the company's mission to organize and then search for an extraordinary range of global information on the Internet to make it universally accessible and useful, Google transformed into one of the most influential worldwide technology firms.

MTV has long embraced a unique hiring strategy, often recruiting individuals from their target demographics—even for senior roles—who possess a deep understanding of the network's audience and cultural trends. This empathetic approach allows MTV to stay at the forefront of youth culture, effectively connecting with its viewers, adapting to ever-changing times, and staying in tune with the latest fashion trends.

The Swatch marketing team's success demonstrates an additional crucial lesson in leadership and team composition: Having the right people at the right time is more important than simply having the same people throughout the entire journey. Swatch's success was achieved through the creative, scrappy efforts of a small, agile team. These individuals were pivotal during the early stages of the company, but as Swatch grew, different leadership styles and capabilities became necessary to sustain its expansion into larger markets.

Tesla's story exemplifies the principle of needing the right leader at the right time. Tesla was founded by Martin Eberhard and Marc Tarpenning, both of whom were instrumental in the company's early development. Eberhard, a visionary engineer, led Tesla through its earliest challenges, from conceptualizing the Tesla Roadster to securing initial funding. However, as Tesla began to scale, it became clear that Eberhard's leadership style was not suited for the company's next phase: global expansion and aggressive growth.

In 2008, Elon Musk, —initially an investor in Tesla—replaced Martin Eberhard as CEO, ushering in a new phase for the company. His bold vision and appetite for risk were critical in steering Tesla from financial uncertainty to a stronger position in the electric vehicle market. Musk raised significant capital, pursued ambitious projects like the Model S and Gigafactories, and reshaped Tesla's trajectory with sweeping changes. This leadership shift mirrors Swatch's own evolution, where early groundwork by Theile and the marketing team was later accelerated by figures like Nicolas Hayek, who, like Musk, were brought in not to preserve the status quo but to drive bold expansion into uncharted territory.

In essence, adaptive leadership is crucial for driving global growth. Early-stage innovators like Thomke at Swatch and Eberhard at Tesla played pivotal roles in laying the foundations of their respective companies. Swatch's lean marketing team positioned the brand as a fashionable accessory, while Tesla's early leadership set the stage for future breakthroughs. As both companies grew, they recognized the need to bring in new talent to address evolving, region-specific challenges and to scale beyond their original capabilities. These cases highlight the importance of dynamic, flexible leadership and team composition that can evolve alongside the organization's goals.

Balance a Global and Local Approach in International Markets

Strength lies in differences, not in similarities.

—Stephen R. Covey

Swatch's success in international markets was largely due to its ability to maintain a consistent core value proposition, while at the same time adapting the marketing strategies to accommodate cultural differences. The brand's central positioning strategy at the intersection of fashion accessory and timepiece stayed uniform across the globe. However, Swatch also recognized the need to tailor tactical elements, such as communication messages and specific product offerings, to suit local preferences and norms.

Even as consumers around the world are becoming increasingly homogeneous in many of their preferences and behaviors, cultural intelligence remains critical for managers and marketers operating in diverse markets. Understanding these nuances and consumer behaviors can help companies avoid cultural faux pas, build strong connections with local audiences, and drive growth.

Theile's international experience and mindset were pivotal for Swatch's global success. In fact, they were one of the key reasons why Thomke had handpicked him for the job. His efforts to ensure the brand name resonated across different cultures and languages, for example, were the result of personal experiences and observations across different markets in which he had lived, noticing where some brand names worked better than others.

This attention to detail demonstrates the importance of considering both global and local issues in business strategy. Companies aiming for global expansion should adopt an international perspective from the outset. In the realm of global marketing, the approach of a corporation to international opportunities is shaped significantly by its management's assumptions and beliefs, and there are four main "worldviews" that are widely considered to influence a global marketing effort: ethnocentric, polycentric, regiocentric, and geocentric orientations.

An ethnocentric orientation assumes that the approach used in the home country will naturally succeed abroad without adaptation, leading to headquarters dictating foreign operations and often neglecting other local market needs. In contrast, a polycentric orientation assumes each country is different, allowing subsidiaries to develop unique strategies tailored to local conditions, fostering responsiveness, but potentially resulting in higher costs and lack of integration. A regiocentric orientation strikes a balance between ethnocentric and polycentric, by focusing on regional strategies. This approach leverages similarities while accommodating differences within a region, such as a U.S. company focusing on EU countries. Finally, a geocentric orientation views the entire world as a potential market, combining elements of ethnocentrism, polycentrism, and regiocentrism to create a unified global strategy that is responsive to local needs without assuming home-country superiority.

Swatch immediately displayed a geocentric orientation in its international strategy. The initial marketing team, though small, was highly effective in creating a cohesive global strategy that could be adapted to various markets. Their background and experience in different countries contributed significantly to this geocentric approach.

Collectively, the Swatch team had a solid understanding of a diversity of local customs and traditions. This multicultural exposure equipped them with the ability to appreciate both the unique and universal aspects of global markets. The team recognized that while the core Swatch brand could remain consistent, the marketing approach needed tailoring to the specific preferences and behaviors of different markets.

In Switzerland, they tapped into national pride by positioning Swatch as a savior of the Swiss watch industry. When expanding to the UK, France, Germany, and the United States, they adopted a flexible yet cohesive strategy. They understood the importance of local expertise, hiring skilled salesmen and country managers to navigate these diverse markets.

In France, for example, the Frenchman brought his innovative ideas and deep understanding of local culture to spearhead a wildly successful PR campaign. Similarly, in the United States, Max Imgrüth utilized his keen sense of American consumer trends to ensure Swatch's designs were appealing to the American market.

The team's ability to adapt and innovate within a unified global strategy typifies the geocentric orientation. They were not bound by a belief in the superiority of their home market; nor did they treat each market as an entirely separate entity. Instead, they struck a balance, recognizing both the similarities and differences across markets and creating a global strategy that was fully responsive to local needs and wants.

This geocentric approach was further reinforced by the team's willingness to take risks and embrace unconventional methods. The limited financial resources and small size of the team pushed them to think creatively and execute high-impact projects on a tight budget.

The approach used by Swatch in its marketing communications worldwide could be described as "glocal advertising": They created a variety of ads that followed a consistent theme but adapted to local tastes and cultural nuances, ensuring that their message resonated across different markets while maintaining a cohesive global brand image. This strategy allowed Swatch to leverage both universal appeal and local relevance, contributing to its global success.

This is an approach used by many highly successful brands around the world. For example, McDonald's tailors its menu and marketing strategies to local tastes and preferences while maintaining its global brand identity. Nike launches global marketing campaigns with localized adaptations that resonate with regional sports cultures and preferences. Starbucks adapts its store ambiance, menu offerings, and marketing promotions to fit local tastes and cultural norms in different countries. And IKEA tailors its product offerings and store layouts to suit local living spaces and cultural preferences, while maintaining its Swedish heritage in global branding. These brands offer excellent examples of successful "glocal" strategies by blending global consistency with local relevance, chiming with consumers across various markets worldwide.

Intuition Can Serve You Well

The only real valuable thing is intuition.

—Albert Einstein

Theile firmly believed that concepts and ideas should first be evaluated through intuition or gut feeling, and only after passing this instinctive test should they undergo rational analysis. He rarely prioritized the reverse order. Placing intuition before rationality was a bold approach, but it served him well at Swatch. Given his considerable experience, it's fair to say that his instincts were well-founded and supported by a strong foundation of knowledge and insight.

Placing rationality above intuition, in Theile's view, ran the risk of stumbling on the same tried-and-tested ideas, which might fail to come up with anything truly novel and creative. For example, Theile's decision to hire the Frenchman based on strong gut feeling, despite initial financial concerns, proved to be a pivotal move for Swatch in that market.

This approach has served other successful leaders in the watch industry. For example, Georges Kern, CEO of Breitling, is celebrated for his transformative leadership. His career trajectory, marked by prior successes at Tag Heuer and IWC, showcases a history of taking bold and innovative approaches. His strategy involves intuitive decision making and prioritizing gut feeling over conventional wisdom. He emphasizes the importance of cultural intuition and personal conviction in steering a brand's evolution. The shift he masterminded to ensure Breitling's traditional macho image was remodeled into a more refined "modern retro" aesthetic illustrates his intuitive grasp of market trends and consumer preferences.

Moreover, Kern's commitment to sustainability, evidenced by initiatives like traceable materials and ecofriendly packaging, reflects an intuitive approach to corporate responsibility. His philosophy underscores the fact that true success in business comes from trusting one's instincts and taking calculated risks, a principle that has been helping Breitling's resurgence in the luxury watch market.

Many other famous leaders across various fields are known for relying heavily on intuition rather than purely rational decision making.

Steve Jobs was renowned for his "sixth sense" in design and product development. The decisions he made often defied conventional market research, instead focusing on creating products that he believed consumers would love, even if they had not articulated such desires themselves.

Richard Branson, the founder of Virgin Group, is known for his adventurous and intuitive approach to business. He often makes decisions based on gut feeling and personal convictions rather than relying solely on market data or analysis.

While primarily known as an investor, Warren Buffett's success is attributed not only to his financial acumen but also to his intuitive understanding of businesses and markets. He famously looks for companies with strong fundamentals and trustworthy management, often making investment decisions based on his first impression of long-term value.

These successful business leaders demonstrate that while rational analysis and data-driven decision making are crucial in business, intuition also plays a significant part in recognizing opportunities, navigating uncertainties, and driving innovation. Their success underscores the importance of balancing rationality with intuitive insights in leadership and entrepreneurship.

This approach is especially significant in the context of entrepreneurship, where personal observation and intuitive reasoning often take precedence over conventional market research. Entrepreneurs frequently rely on their instincts, bypassing traditional methods in favor of a more intuitive approach. According to research by Jeffrey Covin and Dennis Slevin, successful entrepreneurs often adopt a management style that breaks with convention, characterized by three key aspects: risk-taking, innovation, and proactive behavior. Rather than relying on extensive prior research, entrepreneurs often begin with unconventional questions that lead to innovative solutions, underscoring their ability to think outside the box and act decisively. James Dyson, for example, created the bagless vacuum cleaner after observing traditional ones lost suction as the bag filled. Launched in 1993, Dyson's vacuum cleaner became the UK market leader by 1997.

A strong reliance on intuition is often crucial in entrepreneurial marketing, whether in startups or established businesses. Entrepreneurial managers frequently depart from traditional management theories, favoring intuitive decision making over rigid processes. Management scholar Henry Mintzberg introduced the concept of "management by crafting," which emphasizes an emergent approach to strategy formulation. This approach allows strategies to evolve organically through day-to-day experiences and insights rather than being strictly planned in advance. This flexible, intuitive method enables organizations to adapt quickly to market changes, making it particularly effective in dynamic and uncertain environments.

This dichotomy, of course, presents a challenge for academic institutions offering entrepreneurship courses since innate enterprising acumen cannot be easily taught. While the Dysons of the world may not benefit significantly from formal education, enhancing entrepreneurial marketing skills in others remains valuable. The problem is that intuition and gut feeling are harder to teach than rational, data-driven, systematic decision-making processes. Business schools, for example, tend to produce graduates skilled in rational problem-solving, focusing on exploiting opportunities and responding to market changes through data-driven research.

Intuition can be a very valuable tool in decision making, especially when combined with rational analysis. Balancing these two features can provide a comprehensive approach. Numerous studies have delved into the significance of intuition in managerial decision making, highlighting the importance of expert intuition, the influence of contextual variables on intuitive decision making, and the relationship between intuition and rationality in strategic decision making.

Notably, the relevant literature emphasizes that intuition, when grounded in experience and expertise, can be an asset in navigating uncertain and complex business environments. Examining intuition in business decision making and management reveals a spectrum of advantages and disadvantages. Intuition offers speed and efficiency, facilitates pattern recognition, taps into gut feelings, encourages creativity and innovation, and draws on experience. However, it also introduces subjectivity, increases the risk of error, fosters overconfidence, limits accountability, and exhibits variability across cultures and individuals.

While rational analysis and data-driven decision making remain essential in business contexts, intuition can serve as a valuable complementary tool, particularly in situations characterized by ambiguity, time constraints, and complexity. By recognizing the value of intuition, business leaders and managers can leverage their intuitive insights to complement analytical approaches, foster creativity, and make effective decisions in dynamic and uncertain environments.

Coca-Cola's innovation strategy is a good example of blending intuition with data-driven insights. The launch of Coca-Cola Zero responded to an intuitive recognition of shifting consumer preferences toward zero-calorie beverages that still tasted like classic Coke. This was followed by extensive consumer research, including taste tests and market segmentation studies, to refine the product formulation and brand positioning. The result was a highly successful product tailored to a distinct consumer segment, demonstrating how intuition and data can work hand in hand to drive innovation.

When launching the discount airline easyJet, Stelios Haji-Ioannou made a bold move by cutting out travel agencies, relying on his intuition that people would be willing to book flights directly over the phone if it meant saving money. This was a radical departure from industry norms, as nearly all airline sales at the time went through travel agents. Later, he took another risky step by eliminating phone bookings entirely and moving easyJet fully online, despite the Internet still being in its infancy. His instinct told him that online booking would become the dominant channel for travel purchases. While he sought out data to support these ideas, the initial spark came from intuition, demonstrating how visionary thinking combined with strategic validation can drive industry disruption.

A blend of intuition and strategic validation is often the key to entrepreneurial success, balancing visionary foresight with rational analysis. Breakthrough innovations frequently begin with an instinctive belief in a new direction (e.g., identifying shifting consumer preferences or anticipating technological trends). Of course, intuition alone is not enough; entrepreneurs should also reinforce their instincts with data, testing assumptions and refining strategies to maximize impact. In the realm of innovation and disruption, intuition can uncover opportunities that pure rationality might overlook, making it a crucial yet often underappreciated element of decision making. This brings us to the next point.

Rational Strategy-Making Is Overhyped

Markets can remain irrational longer than you can remain solvent.
—John Maynard Keynes

The importance of intuition and entrepreneurial approaches is often underestimated, while rational decision-making processes in strategy tend to be overemphasized. Rational approaches are particularly appealing because decision-makers, especially those lacking deep intuition or original insights, are naturally drawn to tools and frameworks that seem to facilitate "good" decisions.

Indeed, much of the strategic management literature is rooted in the rational (or classical) perspective, which forms the foundation of traditional strategic thought. This approach emphasizes how strategy should be deliberately designed or formulated. Two waves of consensus around this view emerged: the first in the 1960s and the second around 1980.

In the 1960s, strategic planning gained prominence, with scholars like H. Igor Ansoff and Kenneth R. Andrews leading the way. Ansoff, often regarded as the "father of strategic management," introduced the concept of corporate planning, while Andrews, a professor at Harvard Business School, influenced early approaches that led to the popularization of frameworks like SWOT (strengths, weaknesses, opportunities, and threats) analysis.

Andrews' work exemplifies the rational approach to strategy, where effective strategy involves aligning the external environment (opportunities and threats) with internal capabilities (strengths and weaknesses). This approach assumes that strategists are rational individuals capable of logically analyzing both the environment and the organization. Rational strategy emphasizes calculated and analytical thought processes, suggesting that intentional planning is more reliable than intuition.

However, by the 1970s, disillusionment with strategic planning grew as it often failed to deliver satisfactory results. In response, analytical tools like the BCG Matrix and the experience curve emerged to address these shortcomings.

In the early 1980s, Harvard Business School professor Michael Porter introduced his work on competitive advantage and generic strategies, which gained widespread recognition among both practitioners and researchers. Porter arguably represents a second wave of prescriptive strategy formulation. He expanded on the ideas of Andrews and Ansoff, arguing that strategies fit into certain "generic" classifications rather than being uniquely crafted.

Porter's model of competitive industry analysis, particularly his "Five Forces" framework, became a cornerstone of strategic management. According to Porter, formulating an effective competitive strategy requires analyzing the industry, understanding its dynamics, and assessing competitors and the company's position within it. The goal is to identify a defensible position relative to the Five Forces—that is, new entrants, buyer power, supplier power, substitutes, and industry rivalry—and either influence these forces in the company's favor or adapt before competitors do.

Porter identified three generic strategies for achieving long-term competitive advantage: overall cost leadership, differentiation, and focus. He cautioned that a firm trying to engage in multiple strategies without committing to one would be "stuck in the middle," lacking any real competitive advantage and thus becoming a "loser" in its industry.

Swatch, however, presents an interesting case of a brand that appeared to combine multiple competitive strategies (differentiation and cost leadership) without getting stuck in the middle. By leveraging a distinctive and unconventional marketing mix alongside cost efficiencies from mass production and economies of scale, Swatch demonstrated that hybrid strategies could be viable under certain conditions.

While Porter's model remains foundational in strategic thinking and has provided invaluable guidance to generations of managers, it is also inherently prescriptive. It emphasizes a rational, top-down formulation process in which strategy is defined at the senior level and then implemented throughout the organization. These rational approaches, influenced by economic theory, offer practical toolkits for analysis and decision making. However, their application may be more straightforward in smaller or more stable organizations—where information is readily available and decision-making structures are relatively simple—than in larger, dynamic environments. In such complex settings, more adaptive or integrative approaches may complement traditional frameworks more effectively.

While analytical tools and models are vital for intelligent strategic thinking, they must be grounded in a genuine understanding of organizational realities. Strategy formulation rarely follows a purely logical and rational path. Planning and decision making are often influenced by politics, formulation and implementation are intertwined, explicit strategies can lead to inflexibility, and decision-makers may be biased.

To address the limitations of the rational approach to strategy, a number of alternative perspectives emerged, one of which is the configurational approach. This perspective focuses on implementation and the realignment processes required after strategy formulation. Researchers like Gregory Dess, Richard B. Miller, and Miles & Snow contributed to this perspective. Configurational approaches complement the rational view by emphasizing how organizational characteristics should be aligned to support the strategy, offering managers insights into the implementation process. These approaches suggest that structure and strategy combine in specific ways to produce distinct organizational configurations, with planning supporting realignment rather than dictating it.

Another school of thought, processual approaches, offers an additional perspective on strategy. These approaches emphasize the imperfect and intuitive processes of strategy-making, challenging the clear-cut techniques of the rational view. Management scholar Henry Mintzberg developed the concept of "emergent strategy," which posits that strategy often arises from a series of decisions and actions that gradually converge into a pattern. If effective, this pattern may eventually become deliberate.

Mintzberg and his colleague James Waters criticized the separation of formulation and implementation, advocating for a circular process where actions are continuously assessed and adapted as they are implemented. Emergent strategy involves learning and adapting, acknowledging that some strategic elements will remain unrealized. It allows management to delegate control to those with the necessary information, promoting collective action and responsiveness to external cues.

The discipline and practice of strategy have evolved continuously. In the 1990s, a new strategic language emerged, largely influenced by the work of scholars such as Gary Hamel and C.K. Prahalad, who proposed using strategy to reinvent industries by rewriting the rules of the game, rather than simply competing more effectively within existing rules.

Hamel and Prahalad's concept of "strategic intent" emphasized the importance of setting ambitious goals that stretch an organization beyond its current capabilities and resources. This approach forces organizations to be more inventive, making the most of limited resources. Unlike the traditional view of strategy, which focuses on aligning existing resources with current opportunities, strategic intent involves creating a significant misfit between resources and ambitions, challenging the organization to change the rules of the game systematically.

Swatch is a prime example of these principles in action. Thomke's vision was both ambitious and required a significant stretch in terms of technology and overall operations. Similarly, Theile's marketing objectives represented a considerable challenge for the organization, pushing them to innovate and redefine industry standards.

These principles have influenced the development of more recent frameworks and theories, such as "blue ocean" strategy and market-driving innovation. Both advocate creating new market spaces and redefining industry boundaries rather than competing within existing ones. Other emerging perspectives—such as ecosystem strategy, strategic agility, and effectuation theory—emphasize adaptability, co-creation, and the orchestration of broader networks to generate and sustain value. These evolving approaches highlight how innovation, strategic thinking, and responsiveness continue to redefine what strategy means in complex, fast-changing environments. Chapter 8 will explore several of these frameworks in greater detail.

Sources and Further Readings

Andrews, K. R. 1971. *The Concept of Corporate Strategy*. Richard D. Irwin.

Ansoff, I. 1965. *Corporate Strategy: An Analytic Approach to Business Policy for Growth and Expansion*. McGraw-Hill.

Bartlett, C. A., and S. Ghoshal. 1995. "Changing the Role of Top Management: Beyond Strategy to Purpose." Presented at the Proceedings of the Academy of Management Conference, Vancouver, BC, Canada, August 1–5, 1995. Academy of Management.

Bazerman, M. H., and D. A. Moore. 2013. *Judgment in Managerial Decision Making*. 8th ed. Wiley.

Chaston, I. 2013. *Entrepreneurial Marketing*. Sage Publications.

Collins, J. 2001. *Good to Great: Why Some Companies Make the Leap… and Others Don't*. HarperBusiness.

Covin, J. G., and D. P. Slevin. 1989. "Strategic Management of Small Firms in Hostile and Benign Environments." *Strategic Management Journal* 10 (1): 75–87.

Covin, J. G., and D. P. Slevin. 1991. *Strategic Management of Small Firms*. Prentice Hall.

Dane, E., and M. G. Pratt. 2007. "Exploring Intuition and Its Role in Managerial Decision Making." *Academy of Management Review* 32 (1): 33–54.

Deci, E. L., and R. M. Ryan. 2000. "Intrinsic and Extrinsic Motivations: Classic Definitions and New Directions." *Contemporary Educational Psychology* 25 (1): 54–67.

Denning, S. 2018. *The Age of Agile: How Smart Companies Are Transforming the Way Work Gets Done*. Amacom.

Dess, G. G., G. T. Lumpkin, and J. C. Covin. 1997. "Entrepreneurial Strategy Making and Firm Performance: Tests of Contingency and Configurational Models." *Strategic Management Journal* 18 (9): 677–695.

Green, P. E., and W. J. Keegan. 2020. *Global Marketing*. 10th ed. Pearson.

Guzzo, R., and E. Salas. 1995. *Team Effectiveness and Decision Making in Organizations*. Wiley.

Hamel, G., and C. K. Prahalad. 1989. "Strategic Intent." *Harvard Business Review* 67 (3): 63–76.

Harrison, J. K., K. H. Price, and M. P. Bell. 1998. "Beyond Relational Demography: Time and the Effects of Surface-and Deep-Level Diversity on Work Group Cohesion." *Academy of Management Journal* 41 (1): 96–107.

Heifetz, R. A., A. Grashow, and M. Linsky. 2009. *The Practice of Adaptive Leadership: Tools and Tactics for Changing Your Organization and the World*. Harvard Business Press.

Heifetz, R. A., and D. L. Laurie. 2001. "The Work of Leadership." *Harvard Business Review* 75 (1): 124–134.

Hill, C. W. L. 2019. *International Business: Competing in the Global Marketplace.* 12th ed. McGraw-Hill Education.

Hitt, M. A., R. D. Ireland, and R. E. Hoskisson. 2017. *Strategic Management: Concepts and Cases.* 12th ed. Cengage Learning.

Jaworski, B. J., A. K. Kohli, and A. Sahay. 2000. "Market-Driven Versus Driving Markets." *Journal of the Academy of Marketing Science* 28 (1): 45–53.

Kahneman, D. 2011. "Intuition and Reasoning: Two Systems." In *The Oxford Handbook of Organizational Decision Making*, edited by G. P. Hodgkinson and W. H. Starbuck. Oxford University Press.

Keller, R. T. 2001. *Cross-functional Teams: Working with Allies, Enemies, and Other Strangers.* Sage Publications.

Kim, W. C., and R. Mauborgne. 2004. "Blue Ocean Strategy: From Theory to Practice." *California Management Review* 47 (3): 105–121.

Kotler, P., and K. L. Keller. 2016. "Marketing Management and Global Strategies." *Journal of International Marketing* 24 (2): 45–60.

Kouzes, J. M., and B. Z. Posner. 2012. *The Leadership Challenge: How to Make Extraordinary Things Happen in Organizations.* 5th ed. Jossey-Bass.

Larman, C. 2004. *Agile and Iterative Development: A Manager's Guide.* Addison-Wesley.

Lencioni, P. 2002. *The Five Dysfunctions of a Team: A Leadership Fable.* Jossey-Bass.

Linsky, M., and R. A. Heifetz. 2002. *Leadership on the Line: Staying Alive Through the Dangers of Leading.* Harvard Business Press.

Lodish, L. M., S. Morgan, and A. Kallianpur. 2007. *Entrepreneurial Marketing.* Pearson.

Mathieu, J. E., M. T. Maynard, T. L. Rapp, and L. L. Gilson. 2008. "Team Effectiveness 1997–2007: A Review of Recent Advancements and a Glimpse into the Future." *Journal of Management* 34 (3): 410–476.

Miles, R. E., and C. C. Snow. 1978. *Organizational Strategy, Structure, and Process.* McGraw-Hill.

Miller, D. 1987 "Strategy Making and Structure: Analysis and Implications for Performance." *Academy of Management Journal* 30: 7–32.

Mintzberg, H. 1987. "The Strategy Concept I: Five Ps for Strategy." *California Management Review* 30 (1): 11–24.

Mintzberg, H. 1994. "The Fall and Rise of Strategic Planning." *Harvard Business Review* 72 (1): 107–114.

Page, S. E. 2007. *The Difference: How the Power of Diversity Creates Better Groups, Firms, Schools, and Societies.* Princeton University Press.

Porter, M. E. 1985. *Competitive Advantage: Creating and Sustaining Superior Performance.* Free Press.

Serrador, P., and J. K. Pinto. 2015. "Does Agile Work? — A Quantitative Analysis of Agile Project Success." *International Journal of Project Management* 33 (5): 1040–1051.

Spreitzer, G. M. 1995. "Psychological Empowerment in the Workplace: Dimensions, Measurement, and Validation." *Academy of Management Journal* 38 (5): 1442–1465.

Stahl, G. K., M. L. Maznevski, A. Voigt, and K. Jonsen. 2010. "Unravelling the Effects of Cultural Diversity in Teams: A Meta-Analysis of Research on Multicultural Work Groups." *Journal of International Business Studies*, 41 (4): 690–709.

CHAPTER 6

The Marketing Strategy

The very first Swatch collection, launched on March 1, 1983, was a humble beginning, arguably still lacking in style and pizzazz. A meager offering of just 12 watches was far from the bold and daring statement that Swatch would eventually become known for.

Some of these timepieces had been tested in Dallas, Texas, with a limited release of 10,000 of them in October 1982. The results, however, had been far from encouraging. Customers in the test market had exhibited a negative reaction toward the idea, displaying minimal willingness to make a purchase at a price even remotely close to the suggested one.

Theile deliberately chose to turn a blind eye to these findings, fully aware that it was a make-or-break situation. He was well acquainted with the limitations of market research when it came to radical innovation. After all, how could potential customers accurately assess an idea that was completely foreign to them? Their understanding was limited by what they already knew and were familiar with, which may have no relevance to the idea at hand.

For groundbreaking ideas, Theile thought, customers simply could not comprehend or envision how they would function or be used. The ability to visualize the success of a new idea without relying on customer research in the early stages is a tricky marketing skill, making Theile's decision bold and risky.

The earliest timepieces were also hindered by several minor issues. At the launch event in March, a journalist asked whether it was normal for his Swatch Jelly Original to tick so loudly. A hush descended upon the room, all gazes converging on the Swatch team, each reporter holding their Swatch to their ear, listening intently.

With a hint of amusement in his voice, Theile replied: "Well, that is a question we get asked a lot. And let me tell you, it is not just normal, it is a unique feature of our Swatch watches, and actually a sign of the quality of the movement."

The journalists' eyebrows shot up in surprise, murmurs permeating the room. In the early days of Swatch, the ticking indeed proved a problem. This was a technical issue due to the design of the case, which acted as a resonance box, amplifying each movement of the second hand. Despite their best efforts, the Swatch team could not solve the problem in time for the launch in March 1983. So, instead of hiding this potential shortcoming, they embraced it, even turning it into an opportunity. They claimed the loud ticking was a distinctive feature, a sign of the quality and precision of their movement. The Swiss press proved supportive, endorsing the story that "only a real Swatch ticks."

In addition to the unresolved tick-tock issue, Swatch faced a myriad of other challenges. The two most pressing concerns centered around the product itself, demanding swift and effective solutions. The first was the need to quickly identify the most popular designs, followed closely by the challenge of ramping up production to meet the soaring demand for the most successful Swatches—all within the constraints of limited manufacturing capacity. It was a formidable task, to say the least.

With a need for rapid expansion, the production capacity had to escalate with lightning speed, catapulting from a mere 1 million in the inaugural year of 1983 to a staggering 2.5 million by the end of 1984.

Second, the pressure of anticipating the upcoming trends and fashions for the next season was immense. It proved crucial to pinpoint the hues and patterns that would reign supreme. Fortuitously, the Swatch design team was well-versed in the current trends, thanks to their close ties with the fashion world. Their connections, especially those at the renowned Prêt-à-Porter in Paris, provided invaluable insights into what would be deemed trendy and what would fall flat in the following season.

As time passed, the Swatch designs evolved, growing more daring and audacious. Jean Robert and the designers Schmid and Müller infused the brand with a bold and fashionable personality, pushing the boundaries of creativity. Coming up with eye-catching designs often involved a playful and imaginative process, full of trial and error.

As the brand's fame and reputation grew, it attracted renowned and open-minded designers to join their team and pitch new collaboration ideas. One such famous designer was Christian Chapiron, also known as Kiki Picasso, a French postwar and contemporary artist born in 1956. His 1985 design for Swatch is still considered one of the most iconic and sought-after ones available. It was unveiled at the renowned art exhibition "Copy Art" in Paris, instantly becoming a sensation. The style was so successful that today it is one of the most expensive Swatches, trading for a staggering $22,500. It is also known as one of the "Big 5" most collectible Swatches, a testament to its enduring appeal and popularity.

Kiki Picasso's version was only the beginning. Swatch continued to collaborate with renowned artists, including Alfred Hofkunst, Keith Haring, Vivienne Westwood, and Damien Hirst, each bringing their unique flair and style to the brand. These alliances did not come at a hefty price for Swatch in the mid-1980s. Instead, they were seen as wild and imaginative projects, where designers were not paid a fortune for their creativity. With each collaboration, Swatch invoked multiple senses, creating watches that were not only intriguing but also coveted by collectors.

As time went on, new challenges emerged. As Swatch ventured into experimenting with a broader spectrum of vivid hues, they faced the added responsibility of ensuring that these vibrant colors would remain true over time. The engineers had to guarantee that the plastic was stable enough to preserve the original tint—would a red watch retain its bold hue after 6 months, or would navy blue fade to light cyan?

To address these concerns, Swatch undertook nearly 4 months of rigorous product testing before launching a more colorful second collection. Yet, despite their efforts, not all colors proved equally stable, presenting an ongoing challenge in their pursuit of vibrant, lasting designs.

And not every collection was equally successful. Some sold hundreds of thousands of pieces, while others only around 500. In fact, around 30 percent of the designs neither worked nor were commercially successful, but the remaining 70 percent of the designs were met with enthusiasm, selling out in record time.

The Swatch team poured their hearts and souls into every design. But with each success, there were also failures. Designs that did not quite hit the mark left the team feeling defeated and discouraged. It was a constant battle to find the perfect balance between innovation and practicality and between art and commercial success.

Yet, amid all the ups and downs, there were always those few designs that really captured the hearts of the masses to become instant sensations. Those designs made all the hard work and long hours worthwhile; they gave the team a sense of pride and accomplishment.

For the few designs that didn't quite meet expectations, Swatch found a creative way to give them a second life: They were offered as tombola prizes in small Swiss villages, where they delighted and excited their fortunate winners.

Swatch's early product strategy involved distinct product lines tailored to different target audiences.

The initial group comprised individuals who typically wore luxury Swiss watches in their daily lives but sought a more practical option for their leisure activities. These were people who might wear an Omega or Rolex at work but chose a Swatch for sports like sailing, tennis, or water activities, appreciating its durability and lower risk in active settings. Communication and marketing for these basic Swatch collections were limited, the watches featuring two hands, simple colors, with a price tag of CHF 39.50.

The second target segment comprised fashion-forward individuals who gravitated toward the vibrant designs and collections. For this group, Swatch offered more colorful watches with three hands at a cost of CHF 44.90. Among this segment were fashion enthusiasts and readers of popular magazines like *Cosmopolitan* and *Vogue*. They viewed Swatch primarily as a fashion accessory. The target persona for this latter segment was the stylish young woman. Thus, the communication channels and messaging were tailored accordingly.

The third type of Swatch featured three hands and a date display, making it the most expensive model at a selling price of CHF49.90. These Swatches came in blue, black, and green, without any flashy designs, catering to a more sophisticated target market.

In 1983, a Swatch watch with three hands was manufactured at a cost of approximately CHF 16 to 18, as the first million watches were still mostly hand-assembled. Thomke had promised the marketing department CHF 5 for every watch sold, bringing the ex-factory price for wholesalers to CHF 23.

Retailers would pay CHF 28 (allowing for a CHF 5 wholesale margin) before going on to sell it for CHF 49.90, resulting in a CHF 21.90 profit. As mass production took over, the cost per unit eventually decreased to less than CHF 5 per watch, improving the overall profit margin per unit.

Swatch's pricing strategy was atypical in the watch industry. The usual wholesale margin for watches in the mid-price segment was normally around 50 percent. Retailers would then mark up the wholesale price by double. Therefore, a watch with an ex-factory price of CHF 100 usually would have cost the consumer around CHF 300.

While in Switzerland Swatch was positioned primarily as the savior of the Swiss watchmaking industry, other markets positioned it as a fashion accessory showing the time. Swatch realized that competing in the mainstream watch market would mean competing in a mature, hypercompetitive one. Today's strategists and marketers would probably refer to this as a "red ocean" in accordance with Kim and Mourbogne's concept of blue ocean strategy.

In simple terms, a red ocean is a market setting that exhibits intense competition between established players, clearly defined industry boundaries, and limited growth prospects. Competitors try to steal demand from each other, rather than create it. In many ways, by positioning the product as a fashion accessory telling time, Swatch was able to step outside the mainstream to open an entirely new market, an uncontested space where demand was created, rather than fought for—in other words, a "blue ocean." We will discuss this further in Chapter 8.

In its early days, Swatch faced few competitors in the international market, though a handful of small Swiss players attempted to make their mark. These underdog brands were often pushed in supermarkets and department stores like Migros, but they simply couldn't compete with Swatch's success. It would be some time before any serious challengers emerged. Why? Primarily because Swatch had a strong brand and the advantage of being a first mover, making it nearly impossible for others to match its low prices while still producing high-quality watches.

Even when competing watches from Hong Kong entered the market two-and-a-half years after Swatch's launch, they failed to gain traction. Consumers perceived these alternatives as cheap and of lower quality, and, crucially, they lacked the strong branding that Swatch had carefully cultivated. Swatch paid little attention to these competitors, as their product was positioned as a fashion accessory that happened to tell time, not merely as a watch, making the Hong Kong offerings seem irrelevant.

Meanwhile, Japanese watchmakers, who could have posed a significant threat, showed little interest in the market for cheap plastic watches. Instead, they concentrated on digital timepieces and expanded into computer peripherals and IT products. Swatch's marketing team, however, remained vigilant, closely monitoring patent applications from competitors. They understood that even a cursory patent search could provide valuable insights into their rivals' product development strategies and future plans. This proactive approach enabled Swatch to anticipate the Japanese watchmakers' moves, maintain its competitive edge, and stay ahead of the competition.

Swatch's unconventional product strategy, pricing model, and distribution channels positioned it not as just a timepiece, but as a fashion accessory, creating an entirely new market space. This breakaway positioning strategy challenged industry norms and reshaped consumer perceptions, leading to a shift in purchasing criteria and consumption patterns.

However, not everyone was immediately convinced. Retailers were hesitant, notwithstanding consumers being relatively quick to champion the Swatch. Most retailers viewed the whole Swatch idea with doubt, unsure whether it was a saleable one. This may have been because they saw it only as a cheap plastic watch, rather than a stylish fashion accessory. Whatever the reason, it presented a significant task for Swatch's marketing team to convince the retailers to come on board.

One day in early 1983, Theile hopped into his bright green Renault 4—a car that, much like the iconic Swatch, was a marvel of creative design, affordability, mass production, and versatility. Its vibrant green color, like a Swatch on a wrist, made a bold fashion statement against the gray Swiss roads. Theile set off on a 60-mile drive to the charming and historic town of Lucerne, home to the headquarters of Gübelin. For over a century, this traditional family-run business had been synonymous with luxury, renowned as the world's leading diamond merchant. Gübelin catered to an elite clientele, offering exquisite jewelry and top-quality diamonds, making it a beacon of opulence in the industry.

When Thomas Gübelin, the company chief, was introduced to the Swatch, he immediately recognized the innovation behind the concept but felt that Swatch's design and price point clashed with Gübelin's premium brand positioning. Nonetheless, in a friendly gesture of support, Thomas Gübelin ordered 100 Swatches with the intention of offering them as gifts to customers who spent more than CFH 1,000 in his stores. What might have seemed like a minor victory for Swatch turned out to be a significant milestone, as it marked the brand's first inclusion in Switzerland's most renowned premium retailer, setting the stage for its future success.

When Theile met with Bucherer, the second most renowned (and much larger) retailer, he casually dropped that Gübelin was already on board (conveniently glossing over the fact that they were handing them out as free giveaways). Not wanting to be outdone by their rival, Bucherer jumped at the chance, placing a hefty order and agreeing to showcase the Swatch in their stores.

Swatch aimed to secure a spot in the most prestigious department stores, but this was easier said than done. Once again, a mix of coincidence and readiness played a crucial role. Theile was invited to present the Swatch at an annual meeting of the buying association for major department stores in Lausanne. Among those in attendance was Jelmoli, one of Switzerland's most renowned retailers. Recognizing the Swatch's potential, they were eager to give it the global spotlight it deserved. Theile also spoke passionately about the Swatch to representatives from UK-based Selfridges, France's Galeries Lafayette, Germany's Galeria Karstadt, and Japan's Takashimaya. He knew how important a captivating presentation was, firmly believing in the adage "there's no business like showbusiness."

As he spoke, Theile would request two glasses of water—one to drink and the other to put the Swatch into. This simple yet striking action effectively demonstrated the watch's waterproof capabilities. To prove its durability, Theile also liked to throw Swatches out of windows, sometimes from heights of 8 to 10 floors. And every time, the watch remained intact and unscathed, just as the Swatch engineers had promised.

But these acts were not just about showcasing the Swatch's features; Theile wanted to create a memorable experience for his audience. He would end his presentations by giving away a few free watches, allowing the crowd to choose their favorite design. This gesture not only left a lasting impression but also showed Swatch's confidence in their product.

The presentation in Lausanne effectively convinced the purchasing associations. Retailers were assured that the Swatch company would handle all PR and advertising, while the display for the Swatch would be taken care of by department stores. This offered a mutually beneficial arrangement.

However, although the department stores in attendance at the Lausanne conference did make some purchases of Swatch products, the quantities were still minimal. While appreciating the concept, they were not fully convinced of its potential for success. Clearly, the industry was initially doubtful and skeptical of the Swatch, resulting in limited investment in its stock.

Swatch's marketing department had to work tirelessly to win over the Swiss retailers. In the end, it was the undeniable success of Swatch among Swiss consumers that tipped the scales. The marketing campaign in Switzerland was so wildly effective that retailers felt they had no choice but to stock the timepieces. After all, it's always in a retailer's best interest to offer what everyone is clamoring to buy.

Theile's team had been tasked with the ambitious objective of selling 1 million watches in the first year. To achieve this target, they had to figure out the required number of points of sale to move that volume. Through research, they discovered that the average point of sale in Swatch's category sold approximately 2,500 watches annually. As a result, 400 points of sale could trade about 1 million watches in a year. This valuable insight enabled the team to assess the intensity of their distribution strategy. The initial phase involved introducing the Swatch to the European market, first within Switzerland, then to the UK, Germany, France, and, finally, to the United States, all within the same year.

The original plan was to launch Swatch in a new market every 3 to 4 months, but the brand's overwhelming success quickly threw a wrench in those plans. At first, Swatches were mostly handcrafted, limiting daily production to just a few thousand watches. However, as demand skyrocketed, production steadily ramped up to 10,000 and then to 15,000 watches per day. It wasn't until 2 to 3 years after the 1983 launch that Swatch watches were fully mass-produced using machinery.

Swatch's first target for international expansion was the UK, a market that posed a significant challenge due to the stark contrast in fashion preferences between British consumers and those in Switzerland. Additionally, the Swiss watch industry had little influence over British buyers. However, Swatch's fortunes turned when a prominent English wholesaler expressed interest in purchasing 50,000 watches upfront and investing in the venture. This offer was too good to pass up, as it meant securing a business partner willing to champion their innovative concept and help them quickly break into a new market.

Swatch officially debuted in the UK in 1983, with prominent displays in prestigious department stores like Harrods. The response was overwhelming: Swatch sold a staggering 140,000 units in the UK, far exceeding their initial estimate of 60,000. The brand's success was largely driven by its appeal to young consumers who were drawn to the perfect blend of style and Swiss craftsmanship.

After establishing a successful presence in the UK, as previously mentioned, the next countries on Swatch's agenda were France and Germany. The company recognized the significance of entering the French market, given its preeminent role in the fashion industry. France's famous Parisian department stores: Galeries Lafayette, Samaritaine, Printemps, and Le Bon Marché being synonymous with fashion, made it crucial for Swatch to capitalize on this Vogue.

Swatch's subsequent strategic entry into the German market initially targeted Düsseldorf, the country's fashion hub. As Düsseldorf boasted the most opulent boutiques in Germany, it proved imperative for Swatch to establish its presence in this city and its luxury stores, and then, of course, in other famous department stores, such as the KDW in Berlin or the Alsterhaus in Hamburg and the prestigious country-wide Karstadt. In addition, the German market was successfully developed by selecting boutique watch shops.

Despite Swatch's rapid entry into these countries, a thriving black market for their watches formed in areas where they had not yet officially launched. For instance, out of 350,000 units sold in Switzerland, approximately 100,000 were sold on the black market in Italy. The delay in officially entering the Italian market was due to limited stock availability and a focus on competition. The Swatch team had anticipated a fierce response from Japanese watch brands given their success in Europe, thus choosing to delay entry into markets where Swiss brands already held a dominant position. Instead, they prioritized markets that were expected to be more challenging to break into.

Since Swiss watches were already prevalent in both Italy and Spain, and Japanese watchmakers were not as much so in these regions, they were not initially considered top targets in Europe. Swatch had a bold strategy to directly confront their Japanese competitors, who surprisingly did not retaliate, enabling Swatch to quickly establish a strong presence even in markets that were previously dominated by the Japanese.

Theile and his team quickly realized that the first department stores to welcome the Swatch in any given market were not only open to the idea but were also generous enough to introduce it to their colleagues in other stores. This knock-on effect offered the Swatch marketing team the insight that getting just one major store on board was the crucial first step in infiltrating any new market. This store would then act as a gateway, opening the door to others, often through personal connections.

Winning the trust of that first store in a new country was no easy feat—it required a mix of luck and relentless effort. Nowhere was this challenge more evident than in the U.S. market. Despite bringing on board a former senior Seiko manager—someone believed to have deep insights into the American consumer—things didn't go as planned. It turned out to be one of the rare missteps by Thomke, as the U.S. market proved to be a tough nut to crack, leading to significant losses. Eventually, the responsibility for developing this challenging market was handed over to ETA's marketing team.

One day in June 1983, Thomke's voice boomed through the building as he summoned Theile to come to his office. Theile's heart thudded with anticipation as he walked down the hallway, wondering what the urgent meeting could be about. As he entered the office, Thomke wasted no time in getting to the point. "I need you to fly to the U.S. immediately," he instructed in a serious and urgent tone. "We need to secure distribution in that key market as soon as possible."

Theile's mind raced as he absorbed the news. This would be his first trip to the United States—a country he knew little about. A whirlwind of emotions surged within him: optimism, excitement, and curiosity. Yet, amid the uncertainty, he felt confident. He knew he could rely on Max Imgrüth, recently hired by Thomke to navigate this crucial market.

As Theile returned to his desk, his assistant asked him which flight and hotel she should book. Without missing a beat, Theile replied, "Swissair and the Waldorf Astoria." The truth was, he knew nothing about New York hotels. In fact, his only knowledge of the Waldorf Astoria came from old American gangster movies. For all he knew, the hotel might not even exist anymore—but that was a minor detail. The next day, he boarded a plane to New York, brimming with a mix of excitement and curiosity.

The bustling streets of New York soon enveloped Theile after he stepped off the plane. The cacophony of sounds, the rich palette of colors, and mingling of scents overwhelmed his senses. He could not help but feel a surge of fascination coursing through his veins. Although already well-traveled in his youth, the young Swiss manager still felt like a small fish in a big, unfamiliar pond. America was different from anything Theile had seen before. He was ready to dive in and explore this new world.

As he made his way to the luxurious Waldorf Astoria, Theile decided to stop at a McDonald's for a quick bite. The moment he walked in, he was greeted by the friendliest staff he had ever encountered. The lady behind the counter welcomed him like an old friend with a booming, "Welcome to McDonald's! How's your day going?" Her wide smile and seemingly genuine interest instantly warmed his heart. Before he could even muster a response, she had already moved on, greeting the next customers with the same infectious enthusiasm. Theile couldn't help but chuckle at the experience—this was a level of service and cheerfulness he wasn't quite used to.

This first trip to the United States involved a whirlwind of meetings, sales pitches, and new experiences. Theile was constantly in awe of the country's boundless energy and diversity. As he retreated to his hotel room every night, he could not help but reflect on how much he had learned and grown in such a short amount of time. Above all, he was grateful for the opportunity to see the country he had only ever heard about in movies. The trip would leave a profound impact on him, both personally and professionally.

Despite facing countless rejections and setbacks, he persisted in his pursuit of that elusive first order from an American department store which would open doors to all the other stores through their contacts. But, as he soon discovered, this was far from straightforward.

The department stores at the top of list Theile and Imgrüth compiled were the prestigious Macy's, Bloomingdale's, and Saks—but none of these stores showed any interest in meeting with them. Their calls went unanswered, and they were left feeling disheartened and defeated.

However, they refused to let these rejections get them down. During one particularly disastrous pitch, Theile, in a moment of sheer desperation (or perhaps inspired lunacy), hurled a Swatch out the window of a skyscraper. The watch plummeted 200 feet, narrowly missing an unsuspecting pedestrian below. Miraculously, as promised, the watch still ticked on—but even that death-defying demonstration wasn't enough to seal the deal. Turns out, proving your product's durability by nearly cracking someone's head doesn't always translate into sales!

As he left the meeting, shaken and disheartened, Theile's mind was already racing to his next appointment. He and Imgrüth were headed to B. Altman and Company, a high-end department store with a flagship location on Fifth Avenue and 34th Street in Midtown Manhattan. Though their hopes weren't particularly high, they figured it was worth a shot.

As they stepped into the grand and imposing B. Altman & Co., Theile was immediately struck by the opulence of the place. The marble floors gleamed beneath his feet, and chandeliers sparkled overhead, casting a warm, golden glow throughout the atrium. But it wasn't just the lavish surroundings that caught his attention—it was the young woman named Heidi who greeted them. She was the watch buyer for Altman, and as they shook hands, Theile couldn't help but notice the confidence and poise in her demeanor.

What a coincidence, he mused to himself. Heidi, with her strong and capable presence, shared the same name as the unforgettable protagonist of one of Switzerland's most beloved literary works. The Heidi of the novel had won hearts worldwide with her endearing innocence and unwavering spirit. Theile couldn't help but wonder if this meeting with Altman's own Heidi might bring a touch of that same Swiss magic to their pitch.

Intrigued, Theile couldn't resist asking if this Heidi had any connection to the Swiss Alps, the setting of the beloved tale. Of course, she did not, but the fact that her name was the same as that of the famous Swiss literary character proved enough to spark a charming conversation and a serendipitous connection between the two of them.

Their meeting went wonderfully well, with Heidi's keen eye for watches impressing Theile and leading to a substantial order from Altman. But that was just the beginning. Heidi also had close personal connections with the watch buyers at Macy's, Bloomingdale's, and Saks. With a few quick phone calls, she arranged meetings with all three department stores, and after a few meetings, big orders started pouring in.

As Theile reflected on this unexpected turn of events, he couldn't help but feel grateful for his encounter with Heidi. Not only had she helped him secure several major distribution deals, but she had also reminded him of the power of serendipity, storytelling, and human connections.

So, the journey of Swatch's expansion into international markets was marked by both challenges and triumphs, reflecting the dynamic landscape of the global watch industry. With the vision of positioning Swatch as a fashion accessory showing time, the company embarked on a strategic distribution strategy, targeting prestigious department stores and retailers in key markets. From Switzerland to the UK, France, Germany, and the United States, Swatch meticulously navigated the complexities of each local market, leveraging partnerships and innovative presentations to secure distribution deals. Despite initial hesitancy from retailers, Swatch's remarkable success in Switzerland paved the way for broader acceptance and demand.

As the company continued to expand its outreach, it encountered unexpected obstacles, particularly in the unfamiliar U.S. market. However, through perseverance, strategic partnerships, and a stroke of serendipity, Swatch overcame these challenges.

Swatch's success wasn't just about the watches and the retailers. It was also about the story they told and the way they told it. A revolutionary communication strategy played a pivotal role, with early forays into unconventional advertising and PR stunts that would come to define the brand's identity. Swatch was blazing trails in marketing communications long before terms like "guerrilla marketing" and "viral marketing" became buzzwords. In the next chapter, we'll dive into the clever and daring campaigns that captured imaginations and propelled Swatch into the global spotlight.

Commentary and Managerial Insights

Embrace and Reframe Challenges

The optimist sees opportunity in every danger; the pessimist sees danger in every opportunity.

—Winston Churchill

A pivotal factor in the marketing team's success likely stemmed from their fresh perspectives and lack of entrenched experience within the watch industry. Unburdened by its conventions, they introduced innovative strategies that positioned Swatch as something entirely new. Free from the blinders often worn by industry veterans, they approached their task with a boldness and creativity that set them apart.

When watch industry consultants came knocking, the Swatch marketing team swiftly dismissed their advice. They weren't interested in conforming to industry norms or launching just another watch. Their goal was to pioneer a new category: a stylish time-telling accessory that competed in the fashion market, a space brimming with potential for innovation.

Their youthful exuberance and optimism, though born from a lack of industry experience, proved to be both a strength and a vulnerability. Their relative inexperience gave their assessments a certain innocence, viewing every challenge through a "glass half full" lens. This audacity often led them to make decisions that, in hindsight, carried more risk than they probably realized. But it was this very optimism that propelled them forward; they embraced challenges with an unwavering belief in their potential success.

Take their foray into the U.S. market, for instance. They boldly applied the same advertising strategy that had worked in Europe, despite widespread skepticism. Their approach defied conventional wisdom, but their steadfast belief ultimately vindicated their decision.

Swatch's story also serves as a stark reminder that chaos can be beautiful and inspiring. While retrospectives of the Swatch launch often depict a meticulously planned and executed strategy, the reality often veered into chaos. Despite the countless articles and business school case studies that have been published lauding the launch's apparent rationality and systematic approach, chaos frequently reigned.

The Swatch project's complexity, compounded by stringent time constraints and limited financial resources, frequently plunged the endeavor into disarray. Yet, amid the chaos, the Swatch team found order, inspiration, and innovation. They navigated turbulent waters with a blend of common sense, intuition, vision, optimism, and trust in key partnerships, particularly with their marketing partners around the world.

This pragmatic approach bore fruit, for example, in tailoring communication strategies to suit the cultural nuances of different countries like France and Germany. A good illustration was their collaboration with the Parisian PR agency, resulting in a serialized story in "Le Monde." Initially met with skepticism by Theile's team when pitched by the agency, the series captivated French readers, fostering immense brand awareness.

Theile, a self-proclaimed optimist, provides a compelling perspective for exploring the role of optimism and pessimism in business and management. Research on these cognitive biases sheds light on how they influence decision-making processes and outcomes. In essence, optimism and pessimism each offer distinct advantages and disadvantages. Optimism drives reward-seeking behavior, fosters resilience, and encourages taking risks, making it valuable for motivation, leadership, and pursuing long-term goals. However, it can also lead to overconfidence, underestimating risks, and overlooking potential challenges. Pessimism, on the other hand, promotes careful planning, risk management, and realistic appraisal, which are crucial for crisis management and avoiding reckless decisions. Yet it can also result in missed opportunities, reduced motivation, and an excessive focus on negative outcomes.

In business management, while both perspectives have their place, optimistic biases often prove more beneficial for things like creativity, innovation, and entrepreneurship. Optimism can fuel the boldness and creativity needed to drive new ideas, take calculated risks, and inspire teams to overcome obstacles. Entrepreneurs and innovators, in particular, thrive on the belief that they can achieve their goals despite challenges.

Swatch's team embodied an optimistic approach in their decision making, often viewing challenges as opportunities. During the quartz crisis of the 1980s, while many saw the downturn in traditional watch sales as a threat, Swatch identified it as a chance to innovate. And even when faced with skepticism and challenges, like the loud ticking of their watches, they didn't shy away. Instead, they reframed the issue as a hall-mark of quality.

This approach underscores a useful strategy for businesses: instead of concealing or downplaying imperfections, embracing them and rebrand-ing them as strengths can create a distinct market advantage. What may initially appear as a flaw can be repositioned as an innovative feature, or even a sign of authenticity, transforming a potential weakness into a com-pelling unique selling proposition.

We have already discussed the importance of resilience in business, especially with innovative products. Swatch experienced numerous design failures, with around a third not achieving commercial success. How-ever, their persistence in refining and introducing new designs eventually paid off. Entrepreneurs must be prepared for setbacks, viewing failures as opportunities for learning and improvement—a mindset that clearly contributed to Swatch's success.

When Gübelin initially placed a very small order for Swatch watches to hand out as free giveaways, the Swatch team saw this not as a setback but as an opportunity. They leveraged this small win to their advantage, harnessing it for entry into Bucherer. This strategic move also highlights the importance of capitalizing on initial successes (no matter how small or disappointing) to then enhance credibility and broaden market reach. By positioning Gübelin as a valued partner in their approach to Bucherer, Swatch intelligently tapped into the competitive dynamics between these retailers, ultimately securing a substantial order and display of commit-ment from Bucherer.

One effective way to transform potential weaknesses into strengths is by embracing a transparency strategy. Take McDonald's, for instance. Faced with growing criticism over the health impacts of fast food—particularly its high-calorie, low-nutrition menu items—McDonald's could have ignored these concerns. Instead, the company took proactive steps to address them. By introducing healthier menu options, providing nutritional information, and promoting active lifestyles, McDonald's not only responded to criticism but also turned its perceived weakness into a strength, positioning itself as a leader in corporate responsibility and consumer trust. This helped to shift consumer perceptions away from the notion that their food was unhealthy.

In 2014, McDonald's took transparency to the next level with the launch of the "Your Food, Our Questions" initiative. This campaign invited customers to ask any questions they had about McDonald's food, with the company committing to answer them publicly. Initially seen as a risky move that could backfire, the initiative instead proved to be a brilliant strategy for combating widespread skepticism and rumors about the quality and origins of McDonald's products.

By providing detailed, genuine, and comprehensive responses—supported by videos, infographics, and behind-the-scenes content—McDonald's tackled common myths head-on, addressing concerns about issues like pink slime and synthetic ingredients. With input from food scientists, nutritionists, and suppliers, the answers were credible, informative, and engaging. This customer-centric approach not only built trust but also demonstrated that McDonald's valued and respected its customers' concerns.

The campaign's success was evident: It generated millions of online interactions, exceeding its initial question target by 400 percent within just 6 months. As a result, food perception and brand metrics improved, and monthly store visits increased by 50 percent. This initiative illustrates that transparency, when paired with effective communication, can turn potential PR risks into opportunities for building stronger relationships with consumers.

This example highlights the strategic power of brand transparency. Forward-thinking managers increasingly recognize the value of providing accessible and unbiased information to customers, which can lead to reduced price sensitivity, stronger customer loyalty, and, ultimately, a more resilient market position. Transparency involves making objective and truthful brand-related information readily available to customers. This can be achieved through strategies such as encouraging customer feedback and reviews on the company's website, offering honest comparisons of the company's products and services against competitors, and publishing genuine benchmark data, even when it isn't entirely favorable.

Research indicates that customers are willing to pay more and show greater loyalty to transparent brands. To effectively implement transparency, the information provided must be easily accessible, comprehensible, and objective; avoiding the temptation to exaggerate positives while downplaying negatives. A robust transparency strategy, therefore, must be rooted in integrity and honesty.

Studies in marketing have also identified a curious phenomenon known as the "blemishing effect," where including a small amount of negative information alongside a positive description of a product or service can actually increase consumer favorability. This suggests that companies should avoid solely emphasizing positive attributes and, instead, consider a more balanced approach that acknowledges minor flaws. By doing so, companies enhance their perceived authenticity and credibility.

Openly admitting to minor issues and drawbacks demonstrates a commitment to transparency and builds trust with consumers, ultimately enhancing the overall appeal of the brand. Furthermore, strategically leveraging the blemishing effect can help companies differentiate themselves from competitors by showing a willingness to address shortcomings and prioritize customer satisfaction. Embracing this nuanced approach to product presentation can lead to more positive consumer perceptions, greater brand authenticity, and increased market success.

Stop Asking Customers What They Want

> *People don't know what they want until you show it to them.*
>
> —Steve Jobs

Market research is often ineffective for radical innovations because they introduce entirely new concepts or disrupt existing markets in unexpected ways, rendering traditional data and consumer feedback unreliable. These innovations typically lack historical precedent, making it difficult to predict consumer response or assess market viability accurately.

Breakthrough innovations often stem from the innovative perspective of visionaries, who anticipate unmet needs or opportunities, challenging conventional market wisdom and redefining industry norms. Therefore, while traditional market research (for example, in the form of surveys and focus groups) remains valuable for incremental improvements, it may be inadequate for guiding the development and adoption of radical innovations, which require greater emphasis on creativity, vision, and experimentation.

When the fax machine was first invented, the initial market research findings were not very encouraging, and many people did not understand its potential. This initial hesitation and lack of understanding illustrate a common challenge with introducing new technology: Consumers and businesses often find it difficult to grasp the benefits of a technology that requires a shift in established processes and behaviors.

Similarly, when the first personal computers were introduced, many people could not see the need for them in households. IBM executives initially doubted the market potential for personal computers, thinking they would only be of interest to hobbyists. However, as software applications expanded and prices dropped, personal computers became an essential and ubiquitous household item.

When Apple introduced the first iPhone in 2007, many industry experts and consumers were skeptical about its potential. At the time, BlackBerry and other mobile phones with physical keyboards dominated the market, and the idea of a phone with a touchscreen interface was seen as novel but unnecessary. Steve Ballmer, then CEO of Microsoft, famously dismissed the iPhone, predicting it would not gain significant market share, and initial market research reflected this skepticism.

However, as software ecosystems grew, apps became more varied, and prices became more affordable, the iPhone—and smartphones overall—evolved into indispensable tools for daily life. The touchscreen interface, once an unusual feature, became the norm, and the combination of multiple functions into one device revolutionized how people communicate, work, and entertain themselves.

The eventual success of the fax machine, personal computer, and iPhone demonstrates that while market research might initially suggest limited interest or understanding, this can change as the broader technological and social environment evolves. Innovators must sometimes push forward despite early skepticism, especially if they believe that their technology addresses a latent need or can create new efficiencies and conveniences.

Traditional market research methods are often based on existing consumer behaviors and preferences, which may not be applicable to entirely new products. When Swatch's initial market tests in Dallas yielded negative results, the leadership team understood that consumers could not fully grasp the concept of a fashionable, affordable Swiss watch.

Entrepreneurs should acknowledge that while market research is valuable, it has its limits, especially for products that defy conventional categories. Swatch's approach of directly observing and engaging with customers, such as talking to them outside department stores, highlights the significance of understanding consumer behavior at a granular level. This hands-on approach provided Swatch with valuable insights into purchase decisions, preferences, and pain points, enabling them to tailor their marketing strategies accordingly. For managers and marketers, this underscores the importance of investing time and resources into activities that allow direct interaction with customers.

In essence, customers did not realize that they needed a Swatch watch until it was made available to them. The Swatch concept was so revolutionary that it could only be understood by seeing it and using it. Instead of relying solely on surveys and focus groups, the marketing team had to use their intuition, vision, and customer observation to understand customer preferences. By immersing themselves in the lives of potential customers, the Swatch team were able to uncover hidden needs and desires, leading to a unique product. This highlights the importance for marketers to spend time with customers outside of the office.

The key takeaway is that effective market research should focus on identifying the underlying problems customers face or the outcomes they are aiming to achieve, rather than directly asking them what solutions they need. This approach aligns with Clayton Christensen's "jobs to be done" theory, which suggests that customers "hire" products or services to fulfill specific tasks or meet particular needs in their lives. Every product, in essence, is just a tool to get a job done.

For instance, when someone buys a smartphone, they aren't merely purchasing a device; they are "hiring" it to stay connected with loved ones, access information on the go, and capture and share memories through photos and videos. Similarly, a person subscribing to a streaming service like Netflix is "hiring" it for entertainment and relaxation after a long day, while someone buying a fitness tracker is seeking the benefits of monitoring their activity levels and improving their health. In a business context, a company might "hire" accounting software to streamline financial management, and a restaurant might "hire" a food delivery service to reach more customers.

By focusing on the "jobs" customers are trying to accomplish, businesses can tailor their offerings to better meet these needs, developing solutions that directly address specific pain points or desired outcomes. This customer-centric approach not only fosters innovation but also strengthens the value proposition of products and services in the marketplace.

Therefore, instead of asking customers what features or solutions they want, effective market research should delve into the context, circumstances, and challenges they encounter. By understanding the underlying problems customers are trying to solve, companies can gain deeper insights into their motivations and preferences. Armed with this understanding, businesses can then apply their expertise and creativity to develop innovative solutions that truly address customer needs and deliver real value.

Christensen's research highlights the importance of looking beyond surface-level feedback to uncover the root causes of customer dissatisfaction or unmet needs. This allows companies to create products and services that resonate deeply with their target market. Good market research focuses on identifying the problems customers face or the outcomes they want to achieve, rather than asking them to suggest solutions. Then it's the company's job to develop the right solutions based on these insights. That's what makes market research truly effective and products more likely to be successful.

To achieve this, more companies are turning to ethnography: a research method that involves extended fieldwork and participant observation, much like the techniques anthropologists use to study human behavior. In essence, it entails observing people, rather than asking them a bunch of questions. This approach provides a deeper understanding of how individuals interact with their environment and highlights the discrepancies between what people say and what they actually do. By immersing themselves in the everyday activities of customers, companies can uncover critical insights into their true needs and behaviors, often identifying problems that customers themselves may not even realize they have.

The roots of marketing ethnography can be traced back to Xerox in 1982, when the company faced challenges with a complex photocopier that users found difficult to operate. To uncover the underlying issues, anthropologists installed cameras to observe workers in action. These observations led to significant changes in product design, including the introduction of the now-standard big green button on copy machines, which was a direct result of realizing the need to simplify the process for the casual photocopier user. This pivotal insight underscored the importance of a user-cantered approach, making technology more accessible and intuitive.

This pioneering use of ethnography in business marked a shift toward deeper, more empathetic understanding of customer experiences. This success prompted other companies to adopt ethnography in various industries. In today's competitive markets, innovation and an understanding of customer needs are crucial. Ethnographic research can aid in product design, target market selection, innovation, and understanding unfamiliar markets.

Ethnographic market research also has its drawbacks. It can take more time and money than traditional methods and create unstructured data that require interpretation. Some consider it an interpretative and subjective approach, which lacks validity and credibility, and is thus unable to produce generalizable statistical analyses. Despite these criticisms, many companies have found that ethnographic research can offer unique and powerful insights.

Procter & Gamble (P&G) used ethnographic methods to innovate their Pampers diaper line. Researchers spent extensive time with mothers, observing their routines and understanding the challenges they faced with existing diapers. Insights from these observations led to the design of diapers that were more absorbent and fit better, addressing the specific needs of both babies and parents.

Intel's anthropologists conducted fieldwork in Chinese households to understand how people interacted with technology. They discovered that many users preferred tablets to laptops due to their portability and ease of use for watching videos and browsing the Internet. These insights influenced Intel's product development strategy in the Chinese market, leading to devices that better matched consumer preferences.

IKEA employs ethnographic research to understand how people live and use furniture in their homes. Researchers visit customers' homes around the world to observe their living conditions and interactions with furniture. This deep understanding informs the design of functional, stylish, and affordable furniture that meets the diverse needs of customers globally.

In today's entrepreneurial landscape, co-creation has become a powerful tool for discovering and validating new products. Rather than treating customers as passive consumers of a finished product, co-creation actively involves them in the development process. This approach allows companies to refine their ideas with direct input from the very people who will use the product, ensuring a better market fit from the outset.

A notable example of this is Lego's Ideas platform, where fans can submit and vote on new Lego sets. The "Women of NASA" set, a successful product, emerged from this model of co-creation. By engaging users early in the process, Lego ensured that new products had proven demand before launch. Similarly, Swatch, though hands-on with its users, might have benefited from a more structured co-creation platform like Lego's. By harnessing early feedback, Swatch could have explored even more creative designs.

Threadless, an online apparel company, built its entire business model around co-creation. Users submit t-shirt designs, and the community votes on which should be produced. This allows Threadless to release only those designs with strong community support, ensuring high demand from the start. If Swatch had had the option of establishing a similar online community, it could have fostered a robust feedback loop, resulting in watch designs with higher initial customer backing.

The Community-Led Model takes co-creation to the next level by engaging passionate users in shaping a product's development. While Swatch successfully tapped into consumer needs, modern companies can now use communities to accelerate this process, crowdsourcing ideas and validating concepts in real-time. These communities create feedback loops that shorten the product discovery phase and enable faster iterations.

For example, GitHub thrives on this model, as developers contribute to the platform's growth by co-creating open-source tools and features. Similarly, Intel used co-creation by sending anthropologists into Chinese households to observe how consumers interacted with technology. They discovered that portability and ease of use were crucial to Chinese users, which led Intel to prioritize tablets.

Co-creation doesn't replace visionary leadership, it complements it. Leaders must balance their creative instincts with the practical insights gained from community engagement. A visionary product can only reach its full potential when it is tested, validated, and co-created with the people who will ultimately use it.

Harness the Power of Effective Storytelling

The most powerful person in the world is the storyteller.

—Steve Jobs

Previously, we discussed the importance of building brand identity as soon as possible, and the two key drivers of brand performance: (1) a strong level of brand awareness and (2) a set of unique, strong, and favorable associations linked to it.

For example, BMW has a strong global presence and is synonymous with performance, engineering excellence, luxury, and driving pleasure. Microsoft is particularly well known for its software products—which benefit from high brand awareness—and the company is associated with technology innovation, reliability, and productivity. Adidas is recognized globally for its high-performance athletic gear, and the company is associated with sports excellence, innovation, and athlete endorsements.

How are these associations formed? The key lies in the art of storytelling, which, when mastered, can elevate a product into a beloved brand. Crafting meaningful brand associations hinges on the ability to tell compelling stories that resonate with customers. As marketing expert Seth Godin once aptly noted, "Marketing is no longer about the stuff that you make, but about the stories you tell." This quote encapsulates the view that successful marketing today is more about creating narratives that resonate with customers rather than just focusing on the product itself. Stories are what create true emotional connections, helping brands stand out in a crowded marketplace.

Storytelling is effective partly due to its powerful psychological and physiological impact. In a recent research paper, neuroscientist Paul J. Zak underscored the significance of storytelling as a vital marketing tool. Zak's research reveals that character-driven narratives trigger the release of oxytocin, a neurochemical that enhances trust and empathy, making stories both persuasive and memorable. He explains that storytelling not only captivates audiences by engaging their attention but also inspires action by building emotional connections. Moreover, storytelling can profoundly influence both external marketing and internal organizational culture by conveying a brand's deeper purpose and values.

So how can brands craft narratives that capture attention, evoke strong emotional and physiological responses, and deeply resonate within the subconscious? The key lies in mastering the timeless art of archetypal storytelling.

Across stories, movies, plays, and even folklore, have you noticed how the same kinds of characters often appear? Archetypal figures like the hero and the villain, the rescuer and the victim, the mentor and the student, or the lover and the beloved, consistently resonate across cultures and eras, deeply connecting with audiences on a universal level.

These recurring character profiles are known as archetypes, fundamental elements in storytelling that evoke deep-seated emotions to connect with universal human experiences. Shakespeare's plays, for instance, are replete with archetypal characters that continue to resonate with audiences today.

Consider Hamlet, the brooding prince grappling with existential questions, or Lady Macbeth, driven by ambition to commit unspeakable acts. Then there is the cunning and manipulative Iago from Othello, and the star-crossed lovers Romeo and Juliet, symbols of tragic romance. These characters embody universal themes and dilemmas that transcend time and culture, illustrating how archetypes enrich storytelling by tapping into fundamental aspects of the human situation.

Swiss psychiatrist Carl Jung was the pioneer in the 1950s behind the concept of psychological archetypes, which he identified as universal characters rooted in the collective unconscious and present in myths across cultures. According to Jung, these archetypes evoke deep, automatic responses in people due to their connection with fundamental human experiences. This inherent familiarity makes them highly effective in storytelling, where they can create resonance and connection with audiences. Jung identified archetypes such as the Hero, the Mother, the Wise Old Man, and the Trickster, each embodying core human motivations and experiences. These archetypes act as timeless symbols that engage our subconscious, enriching stories by tapping into universal themes and emotions.

For marketers, aligning a brand with specific archetypes allows for the harnessing of these powerful narratives to create meaningful connections with consumers. This not only reinforces brand identity but also fosters loyalty. Archetypes thus play a crucial role in how brands communicate their values and resonate with their target audience.

A notable example is P&G's "Thank you, Mom" campaign, which successfully employed the Caregiver archetype. By portraying mothers as nurturing and supportive figures, especially during the high-stress context of the Olympics, P&G reinforced its brand as trustworthy and caring. This narrative deeply resonated with universal emotions of love, sacrifice, and dedication, effectively positioning P&G's products as essential for families worldwide and establishing a powerful emotional connection with consumers.

In 2001, Margaret Mark and Carol S. Pearson introduced a groundbreaking framework that outlined 12 distinct archetypes applicable to brand management. These archetypes (such as the Innocent, the Hero, the Caregiver, and the Explorer) are rooted in fundamental human desires and motivations, making them powerful tools for creating resonant brand identities. Mark, a seasoned marketing strategist, and Pearson, a psychologist, collaborated to bring the principles of Jungian archetypes into the realm of branding. Their work, detailed in the influential book *The Hero and the Outlaw*, offers a comprehensive guide for brands to leverage these universal character types. By aligning a brand with a specific archetype, marketers can tap into deep-seated cultural and psychological associations, crafting narratives that resonate on a subconscious level and triggering innate and subconscious responses in consumers.

According to Mark and Pearson, brands like Nike embody the Hero archetype through narratives of empowerment and triumph, while Coca-Cola taps into the Innocent archetype with messages of nostalgia and joy. Disney utilizes the tagline "Where Dreams Come True" to evoke a sense of wizardry and enchantment, appealing to the Magician archetype. Such strategic alignment with archetypes allows brands to resonate more effectively with their target audience, influencing perceptions and driving brand loyalty.

It is useful for a brand to select and evoke specific archetypes to avoid sending mixed messages and maintain consistency, as consumers value brands that they can trust and predict. Once chosen, the brand archetypes define the brand's personality, influencing every aspect of its presentation to the world, from advertising language and imagery to packaging and customer service. Strong and world-leading brands meticulously craft every detail to convey their archetypes, shaping their entire brand experience to tell a compelling story that resonates with consumers.

While Mark and Pearson originally advocated for brands to evoke a single archetype to avoid diluting their identity, recent research suggests that many brands now successfully evoke multiple archetypes simultaneously in their marketing communications. This modern approach leverages the variety of transmission channels available today, allowing brands to appeal to diverse consumer needs and emotions throughout the customer journey.

By strategically blending selected archetypes, brand managers can embrace the complexity of storytelling, catering to a broader spectrum of consumer preferences and emotions. Identifying complementary archetypal combinations enables the creation of unique, multilayered, and cohesive narratives that maintain consistent messaging while resonating with different segments of the audience. This approach not only enriches the brand's story but also strengthens its ability to connect meaningfully with a wider range of consumers, ensuring both relevance and impact across various touchpoints.

Apple's brand, for example, seems to effortlessly embody multiple archetypes—such as the Creator, Ruler, Magician, and Sage—through its comprehensive marketing strategy. Innovation lies at the core of Apple's identity, aligning it with the Creator archetype. From groundbreaking products like the iPhone and MacBook to pioneering technologies such as Face ID and Touch Bar, Apple continually pushes the boundaries of what is possible in consumer electronics.

Their commitment to innovation not only establishes Apple as a creator of cutting-edge technology but also reinforces its role as a visionary leader in the industry, akin to the Ruler archetype. Apple's retail experience, particularly through its Genius Bar and customer service, reflects the Sage archetype by providing expert guidance and knowledge to customers. This aspect of their marketing strategy not only enhances brand loyalty but also positions Apple as a trusted adviser in technology.

Moreover, Apple's marketing campaigns, such as the iconic "Think Different" and "Shot on iPhone," evoke the Magician archetype by emphasizing the transformative power of technology to inspire creativity and change.

By seamlessly integrating these archetypes into its marketing approach, Apple maintains a cohesive brand narrative that resonates with consumers globally, solidifying its position as a dominant force in both technology innovation and consumer culture.

Swatch also effectively channeled multiple archetypes—notably the Jester, Lover, Magician, and Everyman—through its distinctive marketing strategy. As the Jester archetype, Swatch brought whimsy and playfulness to the watch industry with its colorful and creative designs. Each Swatch timepiece was a statement of individuality and joy, appealing to customers who seek to express their unique personalities through fashion.

The Lover archetype was embodied in Swatch's passionate commitment to craftsmanship and design excellence. Their collaborations with renowned artists and designers, as well as limited-edition collections, reflect a deep appreciation for aesthetics and creativity, resonating with consumers who cherished beauty and artistry in their accessories.

Swatch also portrayed elements of the Magician archetype through its ability to transform a simple timekeeping device into a fashion statement and cultural icon. Through innovative materials, bold designs, and trend-setting styles, Swatch enchanted and captivated its audience, demonstrating the metamorphic power of fashion.

Lastly, Swatch embraced the Everyman archetype by making stylish and reliable timepieces accessible to a wide range of consumers. Whether through affordable pricing, diverse product lines, or inclusive marketing campaigns, Swatch fostered a sense of community and belonging among its global customer base, celebrating the diversity of personal styles and preferences.

Swatch's early success serves as a reminder of the impact that persuasive and memorable presentations can have in captivating and engaging potential partners and clients. Theile's presentations were not merely informative but also deeply engaging, utilizing dramatic demonstrations of the product's features to capture attention. His creative storytelling techniques were instrumental in generating interest and securing buy-in for the brand.

For example, Theile's use of dramatic demonstrations (such as submerging the watch in water or dropping it from heights) vividly showcased the product's waterproof capabilities and durability, leaving a lasting impression on retailers. These tactics effectively communicated the quality and innovation of Swatch, convincing potential buyers of the brand's value. This approach is a valuable lesson for anyone looking to sell a new concept or idea, demonstrating how powerful storytelling and bold demonstrations can differentiate a product and resonate with an audience.

In the world of entrepreneurship and marketing, showmanship (the ability to tell compelling stories and present ideas with flair) is crucial for capturing attention, gaining buy-in, and ultimately selling products. Storytelling can be a powerful tool for entrepreneurs because it transcends mere product features; it creates emotional connections and shapes perceptions. A well-crafted narrative can transform a mundane item into something imbued with meaning and desirability.

Consider, once again, Apple under Steve Jobs' leadership: He was a master storyteller who framed Apple's products not just as technological innovations but as tools to empower creativity and challenge the status quo. The launch of the iPod in 2001, for instance, was not just about a new MP3 player; it was about carrying "a thousand songs in your pocket," revolutionizing how music was consumed and experienced.

Similarly, Airbnb's success can be attributed in part to its founders' ability to weave a compelling narrative. They did not just offer lodging options; they sold the idea of belonging anywhere in the world, fostering cultural exchange and memorable experiences. Their storytelling resonated with travelers seeking more than just a place to stay—it offered a tale of adventure and connection.

For entrepreneurs, storytelling is not only limited to the product itself but also extends to the brand identity, mission, and values. Patagonia, the outdoor apparel company, leverages storytelling to convey its commitment to environmental sustainability and activism. Through campaigns like "Don't Buy This Jacket," Patagonia encourages consumers to rethink their consumption habits and aligns its products with a deeper purpose—a narrative that attracts environmentally conscious customers who value authenticity and ethical practices.

Showmanship enhances storytelling by transforming the delivery of ideas and products into an engaging, memorable experience. It is not just about what is said, but how it is presented—capturing attention, building excitement, and leaving a lasting impression. Few embody this better than Richard Branson, whose Virgin Group spans industries from airlines to music. Branson's persona as a daring entrepreneur is deeply intertwined with Virgin's brand identity. His flair for showmanship—whether through record-breaking adventures or extravagant product launches—reinforces Virgin's reputation for boldness and customer-centric innovation. This theatrical approach helps the brand stand out in competitive markets, strengthening its narrative of challenging conventions and embracing audacious ideas.

Michael O'Leary, the CEO of Ryanair, is renowned for his unabashed showmanship and provocative leadership style within the aviation industry. O'Leary has cultivated a persona characterized by bold statements and sharp wit, with a knack for generating headlines. His approach to business is marked by unconventional strategies, such as the introduction of controversial fees that challenge industry norms. O'Leary's showmanship extends beyond simple publicity stunts; it underscores his commitment to driving efficiencies, cutting costs, and, ultimately, delivering low fares that have reshaped the European airline market. His unapologetic demeanor and theatrical flair have made him a polarizing figure, but, undeniably, they have also contributed to Ryanair's success and O'Leary's reputation as one of the most recognizable personalities in global business.

Effective storytelling is not just confined to product launches or marketing campaigns—it permeates all aspects of brand communication. Dove's "Real Beauty" campaign challenged conventional aesthetic standards by celebrating diversity and promoting self-confidence among women. By telling stories of real women and the uniqueness of their beauty, Dove sparked conversations about societal norms to garner widespread praise for its inclusive approach—an example of how storytelling can drive social change and build brand loyalty.

According to Seth Godin, truly great brand stories have several key characteristics: They are true, make a promise, are trusted, are subtle, happen fast, appeal more to our senses than to logic, are well-targeted, are consistent, and they reinforce existing perceptions.

Swatch exemplifies this approach to storytelling. Its narrative was true and authentic from the start, rooted in the Swiss watchmaking tradition but presented as a fun, fashionable accessory. It promised affordable luxury and style, a bold and audacious claim at the time. The marketing was nontraditional, allowing consumers to draw their own conclusions about Swatch's blend of heritage and innovation. Swatch did not immediately try to appeal to everyone but focused on fashion-forward individuals, creating a loyal and enthusiastic customer base. And by consistently delivering on its promise without contradictions, Swatch reinforced the audience's beliefs about style and quality, making them feel smart and secure in their choices.

In conclusion, the art of storytelling in branding and entrepreneurship is a potent tool that transcends product features to forge deep emotional connections with consumers. By effectively utilizing archetypes and crafting compelling narratives, brands can not only establish strong identities but also resonate with their target audiences on a profound level.

Successful brands understand that authenticity, emotional resonance, and consistent messaging are crucial in captivating attention, driving loyalty, and ultimately shaping consumer perceptions. And some showmanship can further enhance the impact of these narratives by making them memorable and inspiring.

Sources and Further Readings

Arnould, E. J., L. L. Price, and A. Malshe. 2004. "Ethnographic Contributions to Marketing and Consumer Research." *Journal of Marketing Research* 41 (3): 323–337.

Bettencourt, L. A. 2010. "Customer Co-Production in Innovative and Sustainable Practices." *Journal of the Academy of Marketing Science* 38 (1): 84–94.

Beverland, M. B. 2005. "Crafting Brand Authenticity: The Case of Luxury Wines." *Journal of Management Studies* 42 (5): 1003–1029.

Chaiken, S., and D. Maheswaran. 1994. "Heuristic Processing Can Bias Systematic Processing: Effects of Source Credibility, Argument Ambiguity, and Task Importance on Attitude Judgment." *Journal of Personality and Social Psychology* 66 (3): 460–473.

Chesbrough, H. 2006. *Open Innovation: The New Imperative for Creating and Profiting from Technology.* Harvard Business School Press.

Christensen, C. M. 2003. *The Innovator's Dilemma: When New Technologies Cause Great Firms to Fail.* Harvard Business School Press.

Christensen, C. M. 2016. *Competing Against Luck: The Story of Innovation and Customer Choice.* HarperBusiness.

Duffek, B., A. B. Eisingerich, O. Merlo, and G. Lee. 2025. "Authenticity in Influencer Marketing: How Can Influencers and Brands Work Together to Build and Maintain Influencer Authenticity?" *Journal of Marketing.* https://journals.sagepub.com/doi/10.1177/00222429251319786

Ein-Gar, D., B. Shiv, and Z. L. Tormala. 2012. "When Blemishing Leads to Blossoming: The Positive Effect of Negative Information." *Journal of Consumer Research* 38 (5): 846–859.

Fombrun, C. J., and M. Shanley. 1990. "What's in a Name? Reputation Building and Corporate Strategy." *Academy of Management Journal* 33 (2): 233–258.

Fuchs, C., and M. Schreier. 2011. "Customer Empowerment in New Product Development." *Journal of Marketing* 75 (3): 24–41.

Gilmore, J. H., and J. B. Pine. 2007. *Authenticity: What Consumers Really Want.* Harvard Business School Press.

Godin, S. 2005. *All Marketers Are Liars: The Power of Telling Authentic Stories in a Low-Trust World.* Penguin Group.

Govindarajan, V., and C. Trimble. 2010. *The Other Side of Innovation: Solving the Execution Challenge.* Harvard Business Press.

Kelley, T., and D. Kelley. 2013. *Creative Confidence: Unleashing the Creative Potential Within Us All.* New York: Crown Business.

Kotler, P., and K. L. Keller. 2009. "Marketing Management: Showmanship and Customer Engagement." *Journal of Marketing* 73 (4): 10–21.

LeCompte, M., and J. J. Schensul. 2010. *Designing and Conducting Ethnographic Research.* AltaMira Press.

Liu, Y., A. B. Eisingerich, S. Auh, O. Merlo, and H. H. Chun. 2015. "Service Firm Performance Transparency: How, When, and Why Does It Pay Off?" *Journal of Service Research* 18 (4): 451–467.

Luthans, F. 2002. *Organizational Behavior: An Evidence-Based Approach.* McGraw-Hill.

Lyon, T. P., and J. W. Maxwell, 2007. "Corporate Social Responsibility and the Transparency of Corporate Reporting." *Business & Society Review* 112 (2): 163–188.

Mark, M., and C. Pearson. 2001. *The Hero and the Outlaw: Building Extraordinary Brands Through the Power of Archetypes.* McGraw-Hill.

Merlo, O., A. B. Eisingerich, S. Auh, and J. Levstek. 2018. "The Benefits and Implementation of Performance Transparency: The Why and How of Letting Your Customers 'See Through' Your Business." *Business Horizons* 61 (1): 73–84.

Merlo, O., A. B. Eisingerich, D. Gillingwater, and J. Cao. 2017. "The Role of Archetypes in Building Strong Brands." *Business Horizons* 60 (5): 601–611.

Peale, N. V. 2003. *The Power of Positive Thinking*. Prentice Hall.

Prahalad, C. K., and V. Ramaswamy. 2000. "Co-opting Customer Competence." *Harvard Business Review* 78 (1): 79–87.

Prahalad, C. K., and V. Ramaswamy. 2004. *The Future of Competition: Co-Creating Unique Value with Customers*. Harvard Business School Press.

Ramaswamy, V., and K. Ozcan. 2014. "The Co-Creation Paradigm." *Journal of Marketing* 78 (6): 5–14.

Ulwick, A. 2002. "Turn Customer Input into Innovation." *Harvard Business Review* 80 (1): 91-97.

Zak, P. J. 2015. "The Neurobiology of Trust." *Harvard Business Review* 93 (2): 54–61.

CHAPTER 7

Mastering the Message on a Shoestring

Once Swatch had some department and retail stores on board to display their products, marketing to the public came into focus for driving demand. From the outset, the marketing team traveled to various European countries to observe customers' behavior directly and try to ascertain local differences.

Theile's first stops were Germany and Spain. In the latter country, he particularly enjoyed experiencing the culture by visiting various cities, including Madrid, Barcelona, and La Coruna. He approached consumers in person in both these markets, for example, by standing outside department stores, to learn about their purchase decisions, asking questions like: "Why did you buy the watch today? Was it a gift? Did your old watch break?"

Theile was not afraid to be hands-on in the field. The conversations he had helped him better understand customer behavior before presenting the Swatch to retailers. The best marketing often happens away in the areas where products are being sold rather than the office.

Despite facing budget constraints—limited to just CHF 5 per watch—Swatch's marketing team demonstrated remarkable creativity and resourcefulness. Their integrated marketing communications strategy served as a testament to the adage "necessity breeds innovation."

The team's relentless pursuit of impact, coupled with judicious investment decisions, ensured a substantial return on investment thereby cementing Swatch's position as a marketing pioneer in the watch industry. With lofty aspirations of achieving 80 percent brand awareness and capturing a 30 percent market share in the lower subsection of the upper market segment within 3 months, Swatch knew it needed to deploy bold and imaginative advertising campaigns.

Leveraging the traditional media channels available at the time, Swatch launched an all-out assault on consumer consciousness through aggressive and creative advertising. During the first weeks of any market entry, advertisements in the daily newspapers were particularly critical to inform potential customers and promote sales outlets. For Swatch, this approach laid the groundwork for its sizeable market penetration. The team had a clear and ambitious goal: to drive demand and establish itself as a household name in the watch industry.

Beyond the Swatch itself, the Swatch Group also adopted a portfolio approach that maximized the brand's impact across different market segments. While Swatch appealed to younger, trend-driven consumers, other brands within the Swatch Group, such as Omega and Longines, targeted premium and luxury markets. This strategy created a halo effect, where the success of the Swatch enhanced the overall perception of Swiss-made watches, benefiting the Swatch Group's entire brand ecosystem.

Additionally, the Swatch Group's decentralized marketing strategy allowed each brand to craft messaging tailored to its specific audience while maintaining a consistent emphasis on Swiss quality and innovation. This approach not only reinforced the Swatch Group's dominance across multiple tiers of the market but also ensured that its brands complemented rather than cannibalized one another.

In March 1983, Swatch launched their first marketing campaign, flooding the Swiss market with a diverse mix of cinema, TV, and newspaper advertisements. The central message was compelling: Purchasing a Swatch watch was not just a personal acquisition but a contribution to saving the whole Swiss watch industry. The campaign struck a chord with consumers, leading to a swift sell-out of all Swatch watches within just 10 days of its launch. The success was undeniable; demand soared with everyone clamoring to own a piece of the phenomenon. The clientele of Gübelin were beyond elated that they could secure a Swatch for free after their retail store purchases. This led Gübelin to promptly purchase an additional 5,000 units, now selling them to their customers, rather than handing them out for free.

Swatch's initial promotional effort was carried out in collaboration with McCann Erickson, a prominent international advertising agency, and the media procurement was consistently managed in Zurich.

McCann Erickson's Zurich office proved instrumental to the success of the Swatch campaigns. The collaboration yielded a series of highly effective advertising campaigns that catapulted Swatch onto the international stage. From the initial Swiss market launch in March 1983 to subsequent international promotional activity, McCann Erickson orchestrated a symphony of marketing initiatives—ranging from TV and cinema commercials to print media—ensuring that Swatch's messages reverberated far beyond Switzerland's borders, so that they would be picked up by the foreign press.

One of Swatch's most iconic early advertisements featured a bold red Swatch submerged underwater, vividly highlighting its vibrant colors and water-resistant capabilities. This striking imagery, paired with a youthful and carefree vibe, effectively positioned Swatch as a fun, reliable, and stylish Swiss watch brand. The same visual motifs used in Switzerland were then deployed across multiple countries starting in the UK, Germany, and France, challenging cultural norms and transcending geographical boundaries.

In the United States, there was significant skepticism among local advertising partners regarding the potential success of Swatch's campaign, largely due to perceived cultural differences. Many doubted that the campaign would resonate with American audiences. To address these concerns, Swatch's marketing team devised an unconventional approach to test their advertisement before its official launch in America. They took to the lively streets of New York City, offering passersby a refreshing Coke and a delicious burger in exchange for watching the ad. This impromptu focus group yielded overwhelmingly positive feedback, providing Swatch with the confidence to proceed with the campaign in the United States. Not only did the ad strike a chord with American audiences, but it also spared Swatch the substantial $50,000 cost of producing a new advertisement.

Initially, Swatch's campaigns were centered around the watch's water-resistant feature, positioning it as a practical, everyday accessory. However, as the brand evolved, so did its marketing strategy. Later promotions shifted focus from functionality to highlighting Swatch as a stylish fashion statement. In publications like *Vogue* and other fashion magazines, Swatch was no longer just a watch but, rather, a vibrant accessory adding flair to any outfit. This evolution in messaging reflected Swatch's ability to adapt to consumer preferences and market trends.

In addition to its advertising campaigns, Swatch heavily leveraged public relations, organizing extensive press events to engage with journalists from various media outlets. Despite the initial conservatism within Switzerland's PR landscape, Swatch's bold and unconventional approach ultimately paid off, with the brand's vibrant, waterproof watches capturing widespread attention and sparking imagination.

For PR efforts in foreign markets, Swatch consistently employed local teams from each respective nation. This strategy was crucial for gaining a deep understanding of the diverse needs, languages, and cultural nuances of different consumer segments, allowing for the creation of tailored communication messages. Under Theile's leadership, PR teams across various markets were seamlessly connected, fostering a culture of shared learning and best practices.

One of Swatch's early PR triumphs involved the introduction of special blue watches specifically targeted at Swiss bankers. Recognizing the bankers' affinity for blue attire, the PR team cleverly proposed marketing a watch in this color, positioning it as the ultimate accessory for the financial sector. The campaign was strategically designed to appeal to this affluent segment, encouraging them to purchase the Swatch as a way to support the struggling Swiss watch industry. The response was overwhelmingly positive. Major banks eagerly embraced the blue Swatch, with staff from top to mid-level management rushing to acquire one. These bankers not only felt fashionable but also took pride in contributing to the revival of the Swiss watch industry through their purchase.

Swatch's entry into the French market, particularly at the March 1983 Prêt-à-Porter fashion show in Paris, proved to be a pivotal moment that redefined the brand's image from merely functional to fashion-forward. This strategic move, recommended by a Parisian PR agency, marked a significant turning point for Swatch. However, with a limited budget, the Swatch team had to be exceptionally strategic to maximize their impact.

At the Fashion Show, the Swatch team faced an initial setback: The exorbitant cost of exhibition stalls left them with no choice but to settle for a small space inconveniently located next to the toilets—a placement they initially feared would spell disaster. Yet this seemingly undesirable location turned out to be a hidden gem. The toilets were a high-traffic area, with fashion show attendees frequently passing by. As they waited outside, their attention was naturally drawn to the Swatch stall. Curiosity piqued, visitors began to gravitate toward the stall to see what the buzz was about.

To amplify their presence, Swatch also employed a group of young, trendy rollerbladers who zipped around the show wearing multiple watches on their arms. These skaters not only attracted attention but also cleverly directed intrigued attendees with the simple phrase: "Just follow the signs to the toilets!"

This innovative and cost-effective marketing tactic generated immense excitement, placing Swatch squarely in the spotlight. What began as a small stall in a seemingly unfavorable location quickly became the talk of the event, sparking a surge in demand for Swatch's latest designs. This clever strategy not only saved the day but also solidified Swatch's status as a trailblazer in the fashion industry.

Following this successful stunt, numerous fashion brands approached Swatch with requests to feature their watches as accessories in their runway shows, seamlessly coordinating with the clothing designs. The vibrant Swatches, perfectly matched to the outfits, soon graced the pages of prominent fashion magazines. This unexpected opportunity catapulted Swatch into the fashion world, solidifying its position as a legitimate fashion accessory that also told time. The brand quickly became a sought-after item, with photographers, fashion designers, and publications frequently requesting Swatches for various photo shoots. It's important to note that this achievement wasn't just a stroke of luck. The Swatch team's readiness and quick thinking were crucial in turning this opportunity into a defining moment, establishing Swatch as a symbol of style.

One of Swatch's most iconic and audacious PR stunts originated from the unrelenting determination of a young Swiss boy. With a spark of genius in his eyes, this boy was on a mission to pitch his idea to Theile. However, his attempts were consistently thwarted by the ever-efficient Mrs. Balasso, who kept Theile's schedule packed with important meetings. But the boy was not one to give up easily. One evening, he decided to take matters into his own hands and waited in the parking lot, determined to get Theile's attention.

When Theile finally appeared, the boy seized the moment, making an offer he knew Theile couldn't refuse: CHF 100 for his idea, and a signature on a hastily scribbled contract to seal the deal. Intrigued by the boy's determination, Theile, weary from a long day, signed the makeshift contract without much thought and said, "Alright, I'm listening." With excitement shining in his eyes, the boy spread his arms wide and unveiled his idea: "A very big Swatch watch that actually works, hanging from the side of a very big building!"

Theile paused, then grinned, impressed by the boldness of the concept. He handed the boy the promised money and, with a playful gesture, asked him to sign the contract to acknowledge receipt. That night, Theile's mind buzzed with possibilities, and, by the next morning, he and his team were already considering how to bring this ambitious stunt to life. The idea started small, but as their excitement grew, they began targeting taller and taller buildings. Finally, someone asked, "Where are the tallest buildings in Europe?" Within days, Swatch's marketing team was on the phone with Commerzbank in Frankfurt. Only a few weeks later, a colossal, bright yellow Swatch watch, 162 meters long and weighing 13 tons, proudly adorned the side of the bank's skyscraper.

While the concept was brilliant, the execution was a formidable challenge. Swatch agreed to cover the production costs, while Commerzbank took on the task of hanging the massive watch. Swatch had the upper hand, spending only CHF 20,000 on manufacturing—a trivial amount considering the enormous attention it garnered. However, the bank soon realized that suspending this enormous working watch was no simple task. The watch altered wind patterns around the building, creating potential structural risks. The engineering costs to safely hang the watch soared to nearly 10 times what Swatch had spent on making it.

This bold move not only earned Swatch a place in the Guinness Book of Records but also catapulted the brand to instant global recognition, starting in Germany and quickly spreading worldwide. The stunt generated a flood of press coverage, making it a pioneering success in guerrilla and viral marketing. Swatch reaped extraordinary returns with minimal investment, cleverly leveraging its business partners to amplify the impact. The campaign's success inspired similar initiatives across the globe, even making waves on the home turf of Swatch's competitors in Japan. Remarkably, it all began with a determined young boy's imaginative idea, brought to life by Theile's openness to listen.

Another legendary campaign was the launch of a fully white watch, which heralded the dawn of exclusive "limited-edition" collections. However, this actually resulted from a mishap rather than careful and creative planning! One day, Swatch's advertising agency decided to have some fun by painting one of their watches completely white for a photo shoot. Unbeknownst to the Swatch marketing team, a beautiful white Swatch made it onto a TV commercial. When the CEO of ASUAG laid eyes upon it, he became instantly captivated, calling up Theile, and demanding one for himself.

The marketing team was initially baffled when the CEO referenced a white watch in the commercial—they hadn't noticed it at all. Theile asked Mrs. Balasso to locate and play the ad. To their surprise, there it was: a stunning all-white Swatch, prominently displayed. Despite the well-known technical challenge of maintaining a stable white color without it yellowing, the marketing team's quick thinking and optimism spurred them to confidently present the watch as a teaser for an upcoming "Tennis Collection." They assured the CEO, retailers, and press that this collection of white watches would be released as a "limited edition" within 3 months. That was the timeframe Mock had promised them.

This daring move, rather than admitting the accidental inclusion of the white watches in the ad, inadvertently gave birth to Swatch's now-iconic concept of "limited editions." The team hoped that the 3-month window would provide the production team with enough time to overcome the technical hurdles. Fortunately, they succeeded, turning a potential oversight into a major success.

Another remarkable PR campaign from 1983 was Swatch's involvement in the inaugural freestyle snowboarding competition in Wildhaus, Switzerland. Much like the success of the "limited-edition" tennis watch, this event marked a pivotal moment for Swatch in the sports world, as it introduced a dedicated snowboarding watch.

Initially, the Swatch marketing team was approached to sponsor the first snowboarding competition for a modest fee, with the sponsorship lasting just 1 year. However, they shrewdly negotiated a longer-term deal, securing Swatch as the official sponsor of the event for several years. This decision proved to be exceptionally successful, both commercially and in terms of brand visibility. The event grew into a massive popular success, delivering a substantial return on investment and further solidifying

Swatch's reputation in the sports industry. Swatch's association with sports grew, garnering attention from a new target audience, before ultimately paving the way for the launch of the sport collections.

Swatch's marketing strategy during its first 2 years in new markets had to be carefully adapted to accommodate cultural differences. While the core product remained consistent across all countries, the company recognized the necessity of tailoring its marketing approach to reflect varying design preferences. For instance, styles that resonated with German consumers did not always captivate American buyers to the same extent. To address this, Swatch strategically redistributed its designs among markets, directing them to where they would be most successful, while maintaining standardized packaging and pricing.

However, the communication aspect of Swatch's strategy required more nuanced adjustments, as it was heavily influenced by cultural factors. Understanding these subtleties allowed Swatch to build a sustainable competitive advantage by creating relevant differentiation in each market. For example, the communication style in Switzerland differed significantly from that in France or Germany. However, due to limited financial resources, Swatch was often unable to produce customized TV ads for each market, leading to the same ads being broadcast across countries in 1983–1984.

To ensure effective communication, Swatch's Swiss marketing team collaborated closely with both domestic and local PR agencies to develop a unified message. This message was then adapted by local PR teams to align with the language, humor, and cultural norms of each market.

Print media underwent more adaptation than TV ads. The Swatch team discovered some unexpected peculiarities. For instance, *Vogue* Europe and *Vogue* U.S. required minimal changes as their target audiences shared similar behaviors. In contrast, *Cosmopolitan* Europe and *Cosmopolitan* U.S. needed more substantial adjustments, likely due to differences in their respective target audiences.

Swatch's early marketing strategy was a testament to innovation and adaptability. Recognizing the importance of direct customer engagement, Theile and his team made concerted efforts to connect with their audience, gaining invaluable insights into local preferences and purchasing decisions. Despite budgetary constraints, Swatch's marketing team demonstrated remarkable creativity, leveraging traditional media channels alongside pioneering unconventional tactics. From emotionally resonant advertising campaigns to bold PR stunts—such as the iconic Swatch watch hanging from the Frankfurt bank building—the team consistently pushed the boundaries of traditional marketing practices.

Swatch also emerged as a pioneer in guerrilla marketing, employing unconventional and cost-effective tactics to create maximum impact. These included stunts, pop-up events, ambient marketing, and early forms of viral marketing. By adapting their messaging and approaches to reflect cultural nuances and preferences across diverse markets, Swatch successfully cultivated a global presence while maintaining a cohesive brand identity. This emphasis on innovative marketing communications not only established Swatch as an industry trailblazer but also positioned it as a leading fashion accessory brand synonymous with Swiss craftsmanship and style.

Commentary and Managerial Insights

Unlock the Power of Creativity

Creativity is contagious, pass it on.

—Albert Einstein

The marketing team's resourcefulness in maximizing brand exposure with limited financial resources highlights the power of creativity, frugality, and ingenuity in marketing. From strategic partnerships to innovative advertising formats, Swatch demonstrated that effective marketing does not always require a hefty budget but, rather, a keen understanding of how to make the most of resources available. By leveraging creativity to identify unique opportunities and craft compelling narratives, any brand can amplify its message to resonate with their target audience at a deeper level.

Creativity in business goes far beyond product development and advertising; it touches every facet of entrepreneurial efforts. Inventiveness plays a crucial role in problem-solving and decision making, helping businesses tackle complex challenges that often require unconventional solutions. Entrepreneurs, in particular, frequently face intricate problems that demand out-of-the-box thinking. By cultivating a culture of creativity and embracing diverse perspectives, companies can unlock innovative solutions, enabling them to navigate obstacles and seize opportunities in dynamic market environments.

The science of creativity is intricate, involving cognitive processes such as flexibility, divergent thinking, and associative thought patterns (i.e., connecting ideas, concepts, or memories that are not directly related but share some form of similarity or connection). Engaging in creative activities triggers neural processes in the brain that foster the generation of new ideas and connections between seemingly unrelated concepts. These processes are vital for problem-solving and innovation, allowing individuals to explore unconventional solutions and envision novel possibilities. Moreover, creativity has been associated with enhanced psychological well-being and resilience, empowering individuals to adapt and thrive in the face of challenges.

The Swatch story highlights the power of fostering creativity and embracing innovative thinking, demonstrating how managers can unlock new opportunities, navigate complex challenges, and drive sustainable growth. Creativity was undeniably a cornerstone of Swatch's success. The presence of highly creative individuals within the company acted as a catalyst for inspiration, cultivating an environment where innovation flourished and limitations were constantly challenged. This culture of creativity not only fuelled Swatch's rise but also set the stage for enduring prosperity and a legacy of groundbreaking achievements.

Unlocking this creative energy seemed to instill a sense of limitless possibility in the Swatch team, emboldening them to explore uncharted territories until proven otherwise. With a small squad of people and an inadequate budget, generating radical ideas became imperative. The constraints of limited resources necessitated ingenious solutions, pushing the team to extend their creative reach to the fullest.

Swatch's budgetary limitations fuelled a culture where ideas needed to pack a parsimonious punch without overstepping their financial boundaries. Consequently, creativity became the cornerstone of delivering impactful yet cost-effective projects that wielded a substantial influence on their sales trajectory. The most notable examples of these budget-friendly yet impactful endeavors included the prominent Swatch watch on the Commerzbank building and what serendipitously proved to be clever strategic placement of a Swatch stall near the toilets at the Prêt-à-Porter fair in Paris.

Creativity and ingenuity are at the heart of "frugal innovation," a concept that transforms resource constraints into opportunities rather than obstacles. Swatch's marketing strategy in the 1980s perfectly embodies the principles of frugal innovation by demonstrating how to achieve more with less. With limited resources, Swatch revolutionized the watch industry by strategically partnering with the right collaborators, sponsoring unconventional events, and crafting an affordable yet vibrant integrated marketing communications strategy. This approach generated significant consumer excitement, enabling the brand to achieve global recognition without resorting to exorbitant marketing expenditures.

Professor Byron Sharp of the Ehrenberg-Bass Institute for Marketing Science at the University of South Australia argues that there is a critical distinction between being different and being distinctive and that the latter may be more important. Brands that aim to be merely different often introduce minor variations that may not significantly influence consumer perceptions or behavior. These differences typically revolve around unique selling propositions (USPs) intended to stand out from the competition, but they often fail to resonate with customers. In contrast, distinctiveness is about standing out in a memorable and easily recognizable way, which is crucial for consumer brands.

Distinctiveness helps brands cut through the noise of a crowded marketplace, making it easier for consumers to notice, remember, and ultimately choose their products. This distinctiveness is built on creativity—whether through a unique visual identity, packaging, advertising, or other brand elements—that consistently reinforces the brand's identity. By fostering strong, recognizable cues, brands can create mental shortcuts for consumers, ensuring they remain top of the mind when purchasing decisions are made.

Swatch is a prime example of distinctiveness, skillfully creating mental availability (that is, the likelihood that the brand will be top of the mind and easily recalled when needed) through a unique approach to watchmaking and marketing. The brand's colorful, playful, and affordable timepieces stood in stark contrast to the more conservative and expensive offerings of its competitors. This distinctiveness was built on a foundation of creativity, with Swatch introducing a wide variety of designs that appealed to diverse consumer tastes, ensuring there was a Swatch watch for everyone.

Swatch's uniform pricing strategy was a notable departure from industry norms; customers always knew the price of a Swatch watch without needing to ask. The brand's unconventional advertising campaigns, memorable slogans, and eye-catching visuals further helped Swatch carve out a unique space in consumers' minds. This consistent and creative approach made Swatch watches instantly recognizable and easy to recall, significantly enhancing the brand's mental availability. By leveraging distinctiveness, Swatch successfully created a strong, memorable brand identity that truly resonated with consumers.

Make Your Own Luck

Luck is a dividend of sweat. The more you sweat, the luckier you get.
—Ray Kroc

Coming up with ideas is easy. Coming up with good ideas is a little harder. And coming up with good ideas that all market partners understand and buy into is very difficult. The Swatch story serves as a powerful reminder that while a brilliant concept or idea is certainly admirable, its business success ultimately relies on effective marketing and commercialization.

As Thomas Edison famously said, "Genius is one percent inspiration and ninety-nine percent perspiration," highlighting the importance of hard work and determination in achieving success, rather than relying solely on talent or inspiration. The launch of Swatch certainly supports this idea, but Theile reflects on it with an additional twist: "Hard work, yes, but add another 50% good luck!"

Indeed, Swatch, like many other innovations, benefited from a mix of hard work and fortunate circumstances. History is full of examples where chance played a pivotal role—penicillin and Viagra, for instance. Viagra was initially developed by Pfizer as a treatment for hypertension and angina, but an unexpected side effect led to its repurposing as a treatment for erectile dysfunction, ultimately becoming a blockbuster drug. Similarly, penicillin, the first true antibiotic, was discovered by Alexander Fleming in 1928 when he noticed that a mold had contaminated a petri dish of bacteria in his lab, killing the surrounding bacteria. This accidental discovery revolutionized medicine, leading to the development of antibiotics that have since then been saving countless lives.

In Swatch's case, several fortunate events converged to propel its success. The quartz crisis of the 1970s, which destabilized the traditional Swiss watch industry, created a unique opportunity for Swatch to enter the market with its affordable, quartz-powered timepieces. Additionally, the global zeitgeist of the 1980s, characterized by a newfound appreciation for individual expression and vibrant aesthetics, provided the perfect cultural backdrop for Swatch's bold and colorful designs to flourish. These instances of luck, combined with relentless innovation and hard work, played a crucial role in transforming Swatch into a global phenomenon.

The success of Swatch was also intricately linked to the broader economic landscape of the time, with the global market conditions experiencing a fortuitous period of recovery, marked by the stabilization of key economic indicators and the gradual rebound from previous downturns. One noteworthy factor contributing to this worldwide financial ricocheting was the establishment of floating exchange rates, which provided greater flexibility in currency valuations and facilitated international trade.

Moreover, by the mid-1980s, the transition to the electronic era had progressed considerably, with advancements in technology diffusing into various industries, including watchmaking. Swatch capitalized on this technological shift by embracing electronic components and leveraging innovations in quartz movement technology. This allowed Swatch to produce timepieces that were not only more accurate and reliable but also more cost-effective to manufacture, aligning perfectly with the demands of and thus capitalize on this recovering global economy.

Swatch's journey also shows that while luck may seem serendipitous, there is a sense of destiny, arising, as it does, from deliberate actions and calculated decisions. The brand's successful evolution underscores the significance of proactively creating conditions favorable to success and embracing calculated risks to influence positive outcomes. Many pivotal moments in Swatch's success were marked by the marketing team's ability to create opportunities from fortuitous occurrences.

For instance, Theile entering Thomke's office with the intention to resign just as he was seeking someone to head the Swatch marketing team, or encountering Thomas Gübelin in Lucerne, proved to be pivotal moments. Taking a gamble with an enigmatic, untested Frenchman to market into his host country, or heeding the crazy PR stunt idea of a young lad in a Grenchen parking lot, all proved to be transformational.

Even sponsoring a relatively unknown sporting event like the first snowboarding championship, which later soared to great success, was a turning point. So too was the serendipitous encounter with a friendly watch buyer in New York called Heidi. These occurrences significantly contributed to Swatch's success, underscoring the importance of remaining receptive to unexpected opportunities and embracing uncertainty. While meticulous planning and strategic foresight are undoubtedly valuable, they must be balanced with a willingness to adapt as well as a readiness to take advantage of unforeseen circumstances.

It is also worth echoing that none of these opportunities would have materialized had the key people involved spent all their time in an office or in front of a computer (or should we say typewriter?). The Swatch team's success was largely driven by their proactive engagement with the world around them. Their willingness to venture out, meet new people, and explore diverse environments played a critical role in identifying and seizing unique opportunities. From casual conversations to unexpected encounters, the marketing team's dynamic presence in various settings allowed them to gather insights, forge crucial connections, be in the right place at the right time, and be sharp and prepared once there.

This openness to real-world experiences and interactions proved instrumental in transforming abstract ideas into tangible business achievements. It underpins the necessity for business leaders and marketers to step out of their comfort zones, engage with their ecology, by tapping into the consciousness of the surroundings, and be attuned to the serendipities of life that often pave the way for monumental successes.

Businesses can leverage chance through collaboration, experimentation, commitment to a purpose, and the embracing of uncertainty. As Thomas Jefferson once said, "I'm a great believer in luck, and I find the harder I work, the more I have of it," which implies that effort and per-severance create opportunities often mistaken for luck. Similarly, the Roman philosopher Seneca famously remarked: "Luck is what happens when preparation meets opportunity," highlighting the crucial role of preparation in creating what we perceive as luck. This sentiment, much like the story of Swatch, underscores the idea that we have the power to shape our own luck through our readiness, actions, and mindset. By being open to opportunities and taking deliberate steps, we can actively influence the outcomes that others might attribute to mere chance.

Marketing Can Be Frugal

It's not the size of the dog in the fight, it's the size of the fight in the dog.
—Mark Twain

As already noted, despite budgetary constraints, Swatch's marketing team demonstrated remarkable creativity and resourcefulness in their campaigns. By leveraging traditional media channels and orchestrating unconventional PR stunts, Swatch consistently pushed the boundaries of marketing practices.

This underscores the importance of thinking outside the box and experimenting with innovative strategies, particularly for entrepreneurs and marketers operating in competitive industries or with limited resources. Embracing creativity and resourcefulness enables companies to stand out from competitors, capture consumer attention, and enhance brand awareness.

For example, when faced with limited resources for market research, Theile's simple yet effective approach of calling embassies to check for potential negative connotations of the Swatch brand name exemplifies innovative and frugal thinking. This approach not only saved costs but also ensured the brand's global appeal, demonstrating how ingenuity can lead to impactful results even with constrained resources.

In business, constraints often necessitate creative solutions. Managers and entrepreneurs should encourage their teams to find original ways to tackle problems, leveraging existing resources in novel ways or finding low-cost methods to achieve objectives. Swatch's French marketing team's creative solutions, like placing smaller ads in strategic positions and using storytelling in newspapers, allowed the brand to maximize its impact on a tight budget. These innovative approaches captured public attention and built strong brand recognition.

Frugal marketing is a strategic approach that focuses on developing cost-effective and resource-efficient strategies to reach target audiences and achieve business objectives. It involves maximizing the impact of marketing efforts while minimizing costs, making this frugality particularly relevant for businesses operating in resource-constrained environments or targeting price-sensitive consumers. Frugal marketing emphasizes creativity, innovation, and efficiency in designing marketing campaigns, product promotions, and customer engagement initiatives to achieve sustainable growth and competitive advantage. It exemplifies the ingenuity and resourcefulness of entrepreneurs and companies, especially when faced with limited budgets.

For instance, traditional market research methods may require significant financial investment, but frugal marketing leverages creativity and practicality to achieve similar results at a fraction of the cost. One accessible and inexpensive market research method is the utilization of existing resources and networks. Entrepreneurs can tap into their personal and professional connections to gather insights about consumer preferences, needs, and perceptions. Conducting informal surveys or interviews with friends, family members, and acquaintances can provide valuable feedback on product ideas or marketing strategies. Additionally, engaging with online communities and social media platforms allows entrepreneurs to interact directly with potential customers, gather feedback, and test concepts in real-time.

An example of an entrepreneur who effectively leveraged his contacts and personal connections for market research is Brian Chesky, cofounder and CEO of Airbnb. When Chesky and his core team first conceived the idea of renting out air mattresses in their apartment to conference attendees, they initially relied heavily on their personal networks. They began by discussing the concept with friends, family, and acquaintances to validate the idea and gain insights into potential customers' needs and preferences. From there, they expanded their efforts, personally meeting with their initial users and hosts to gather direct feedback and refine the platform.

This hands-on, network-driven approach allowed Chesky and his co-founders to iteratively develop Airbnb based on real user experiences. By staying deeply connected to their community and continuously gathering insights, they ensured that Airbnb met the needs of both guests and hosts. This strategy of using personal connections to guide product development was instrumental in shaping a platform that would go on to revolutionize the travel and hospitality industry.

Another effective strategy for frugal marketing is embracing guerrilla tactics and grassroots initiatives. This approach involves thinking creatively and using unconventional methods to reach target audiences. Organizing local events, street activities, or pop-up shops can generate buzz and attract attention without the need for expensive advertising campaigns. Partnering with complementary businesses or influencers can further extend reach and credibility at minimal cost. By leveraging word-of-mouth marketing and grassroots efforts, entrepreneurs can build meaningful connections with customers while adhering to budget constraints. Swatch executed bold PR stunts in a cost-effective manner. The Commerzbank stunt, for example, generated significant media coverage and public interest with minimal expenditure.

Provocative or disruptive marketing campaigns on social media can be highly effective in capturing attention and conveying a brand's message. By challenging conventional marketing norms with shock value and unexpected visual narratives, these campaigns can create a significant impact. A prime example is Burger King's "Moldy Whopper" campaign. This initiative featured time-lapse videos and photos of a Whopper decomposing over 34 days, dramatically highlighting the absence of artificial preservatives in their food. The bold and unconventional approach generated widespread media attention and sparked public discussion, effectively communicating Burger King's commitment to healthier ingredients while distinguishing the brand in a crowded market. This campaign demonstrates how creative, impactful strategies can powerfully convey brand values and engage audiences in memorable and meaningful ways.

Creative street art or installations can also capture public interest and lead to increased media coverage. For instance, Spotify's interactive billboards, which displayed users' listening habits, generated significant buzz and public engagement by personalizing the experience and making it relatable.

Organizing flash mobs or pop-up events in high-traffic areas can create memorable brand experiences and attract significant attention. YouTube is filled with examples of brands that have effectively utilized these tactics, such as WestJet's "Christmas Miracle" initiative, where they surprised passengers with personalized gifts based on their holiday wishes, creating a heartwarming viral sensation. Another great example is British Airways' singing flash mob at Heathrow airport arrivals, where a choir unexpectedly serenaded passengers with uplifting songs, delighting travelers and creating a shareable, feel-good moment that resonated with audiences. These types of experiential marketing campaigns not only generate buzz and media coverage but also foster strong emotional connections with consumers. By creating surprising and delightful experiences, brands can leave a lasting impression, making them more memorable and increasing the likelihood that consumers will choose them in the future. Effective use of such creative tactics can elevate a brand's visibility and deepen its relationship with its audience. And as the videos documenting these heartwarming events go viral, they can capture the attention of millions and boost brand image.

By combining creativity with thoughtful execution, brands can turn simple ideas into powerful marketing campaigns that resonate with audiences and leave a lasting impact. Partnering with influencers who resonate with the target audience can further expand reach and credibility. Micro-influencers—individuals with a relatively small but highly engaged following, typically between 1,000 and 100,000 followers—offer cost-effective collaboration opportunities. Recent research shows that micro-influencers can be more effective and efficient than larger influencers in engaging their audiences and building brand equity.

Collaborating with complementary brands for co-promotion can also extend reach while sharing marketing costs. The success of Intel's "Intel Inside" campaign is a prime example of this strategy. Intel strategically shared advertising costs with computer manufacturers who agreed to display the "Intel Inside" logo on their products. This cooperative marketing strategy, known as co-op advertising, significantly extended Intel's brand reach without shouldering the entire financial burden of advertising. By incentivizing manufacturers like Dell and HP to prominently feature the "Intel Inside" logo, Intel not only boosted its brand visibility but also established a powerful association between its processors and high-quality computers. This partnership approach effectively amplified the overall impact, making Intel synonymous with reliable and advanced computing technology.

Instead of relying solely on paid advertising, nowadays managers and entrepreneurs can also use content marketing strategies to engage and educate their target market. Creating compelling blog posts, videos, or podcasts showcasing the value proposition of their products or services can build trust and credibility with the audience, ultimately driving organic growth and customer loyalty.

An example where creativity and storytelling captured audience attention is the skincare brand Glossier. Founded by Emily Weiss, Glossier leveraged content marketing to build a strong, loyal customer base. Before launching the brand, Weiss started the beauty blog "Into the Gloss," where she shared detailed beauty routines, product reviews, and interviews with industry insiders. This blog attracted a dedicated following and provided valuable insights into consumer preferences and related trends. When Weiss launched Glossier, she continued to use content marketing to engage with her audience. The company website and social media channels are filled with user-generated content, tutorials, and stories that highlight how real people use their products.

This approach not only builds trust and credibility but also creates a sense of community among customers. By focusing on storytelling and authentic content, Glossier has successfully driven organic growth and customer loyalty without relying heavily on traditional paid advertising.

Many other companies exemplify efficient and effective marketing on the cheap. Dollar Shave Club, for example, launched with a humorous and straightforward video featuring its founder that went viral, generating millions of views and significant brand awareness without a massive advertising budget. By offering a subscription service for razors, Dollar Shave Club built a loyal customer base and ensured recurring revenue, reducing the need for continuous large-scale advertising.

Another example is Old Spice, which brilliantly revitalized its brand through the creative and highly successful "Smell Like a Man" campaign. Instead of investing in a traditional Super Bowl ad—a strategy that, while high-impact, comes with an exorbitant price tag—Old Spice chose a more cost-effective yet equally impactful route: video marketing and social media.

The campaign was ingenious on multiple fronts. First, it cleverly targeted women instead of men, even though Old Spice is a men's grooming product. The central figure of the campaign was a charming, confident male character who was likable to both sexes. The character's humorous and slightly absurd monologues directly addressed women, encouraging them to buy Old Spice for their partners, thus influencing purchase decisions indirectly but powerfully.

Traditionally, Old Spice had been associated with older men, a perception that the brand sought to overturn. The campaign shifted the narrative toward a modern take on masculinity, emphasizing the importance of a man's scent—clean, fresh, and masculine—rather than outdated, toxic notions of macho masculinity. The marketing narrative was infused with eloquent writing and humor, making the campaign both memorable and relatable.

The campaign kicked off with a wildly popular video featuring the now-iconic line, "I'm on a horse," where the male lead humorously implores women to ensure their men don't "smell like a lady." Old Spice also made a strategic move by launching the campaign around the time of the Super Bowl, and buying Google search terms like "Super Bowl advertising." This savvy tactic led many to believe that the campaign was tied to the Super Bowl, thus gaining the prestige and buzz of a Super Bowl ad without the associated costs.

Following this, Old Spice launched an innovative second phase: individualized response videos. These featured the same actor, in character, responding directly to social media posts from consumers. This interactive approach was not only highly engaging but also incredibly cost-effective, allowing the brand to maintain momentum without the need for additional expensive ads.

The overall impact of refreshing the Old Spice image was profound. The campaign not only led to a significant increase in sales and market share but also turned into a viral marketing phenomenon. The success of "Smell Like a Man" earned P&G (the parent company of Old Spice) several prestigious advertising awards, solidifying the campaign's place in marketing history as a masterclass in creative, efficient, and effective brand revitalization.

Nowadays, technology and data analytics can also empower entrepreneurs to make informed decisions and optimize marketing efforts on a shoestring budget. Free or low-cost tools such as Google Analytics, social media analytics platforms, and survey software enable entrepreneurs to track performance metrics, analyze customer behavior, and identify trends without breaking the bank. Data-driven insights allow brands to refine marketing strategies, target specific audience segments, and maximize return on investment.

Today's managers and entrepreneurs can glean valuable insights from Swatch's frugal marketing approach, especially given the broader array of tools and strategies available today. Unlike the 1980s, businesses now have access to a vast range of digital platforms, such as Facebook, Instagram, Twitter, LinkedIn, and TikTok, which offer cost-effective ways to reach large and targeted audiences.

Through engaging content, viral challenges, and influencer collaborations, brands can amplify their messages without significant financial investment. Content marketing, in particular, allows brands to establish a powerful voice and reach by creating valuable, relevant content— such as blogs, videos, and podcasts—that attracts and engages target audiences. Email marketing remains highly effective, enabling direct communication with potential customers. Personalized and targeted email campaigns can drive engagement and conversions at a relatively low cost.

In summary, frugal marketing, exemplified by Swatch and many modern companies, highlights the importance of creativity and ingenuity in achieving marketing success without substantial financial investment. By leveraging digital platforms, guerrilla marketing tactics, strategic partnerships, and data analytics, managers and entrepreneurs can effectively reach and engage their target audiences. The key is to embrace resourcefulness, think outside the box, and create memorable, impactful marketing campaigns that resonate with consumers and drive brand growth.

Be Obsessively Consistent

God is in the details

—Ludwig Mies van der Rohe

The success of Swatch serves as a powerful reminder that an obsession with details is often crucial to a brand's success. Once the marketing team chose to position Swatch not merely as a watch but as a fashion accessory that tells time, they meticulously crafted every element of the marketing mix—product, pricing, communication, and distribution—to align with this vision. Every aspect of their strategy and every touchpoint between the brand and the consumer were carefully designed to ensure that Swatch would be perceived as a fashion accessory, effectively shaping consumer behavior to match that categorization.

Swatch's strategy is an excellent example of breakaway positioning. Breakaway positioning involves distinguishing a product or brand by intentionally deviating from market norms, conventions, or competitors' offerings to create a unique and compelling place in the minds of consumers. Instead of competing directly with established players, this approach carves out a distinct niche or category where the brand can thrive independently. It often entails identifying unmet or underserved customer needs, challenging industry conventions, or introducing disruptive innovations that redefine the value proposition. By doing so, a brand can capture attention, generate excitement, and build a loyal customer base. Breakaway positioning requires creativity, courage, and a willingness to take risks, but when executed effectively, it can yield significant rewards by establishing a strong and memorable brand identity in the marketplace.

One effective way to implement breakaway positioning is by adopting elements of the marketing mix from one product category and applying them in a different context. This strategy can lead to innovative and compelling results. For instance, the low-cost airline Ryanair positions itself at the intersection of air travel and bus transport—combining the speed of a plane with the pricing model of a bus service to offer a distinctly novel value proposition. Similarly, the Simpsons TV show blends the realms of cartoons and adult sitcoms; Cirque du Soleil combines circus artistry with theatrical performance; Airbnb merges hospitality with the sharing economy; and Netflix revolutionized media consumption by combining streaming technology with traditional television and film entertainment. Smartphones, meanwhile, stand at the intersection of mobile phones and computing devices, offering a range of functionalities beyond simple communication.

Breakaway positioning is effective because the elements of the marketing mix act as cues, encouraging consumers to categorize the product in a specific way, which influences their behavior accordingly. By carefully designing these cues, a brand can guide the mental classification process. For instance, Red Bull introduced its energy drinks in sleek, tall cans and stocked them in separate sections within stores, away from traditional soft drinks. These deliberate choices signaled to consumers that Red Bull was not just another soft drink but a product offering a unique energy boost, as emphasized by its iconic slogan, "Red Bull gives you wings." The energy-focused positioning was further reinforced by the can's distinctive design, which was shaped like a fuel tank, subtly suggesting that the drink was a powerful source of fuel for the body.

Similarly, Southwest Airlines exemplified breakaway positioning by departing from traditional airline industry practices. While other carriers focused on amenities, seating classes, and hub-and-spoke routes, Southwest adopted a marketing mix more akin to mass transportation companies. Their strategy included no-frills service, point-to-point routes, competitive pricing, and a communication style characterized by humor and simplicity. This approach not only attracted budget-conscious travelers but also enabled Southwest to establish itself as a formidable competitor in the airline industry.

Swatch employed similar tactics by using cues that were more commonly associated with the fashion accessory category rather than the watch industry. The watches were made of plastic, came in vibrant colors, and featured pop-art designs. Swatch launched its brand at the Paris fashion show rather than a traditional watch fair, and its product strategy included releasing two collections per year, mirroring the seasonal collections of fashion houses. The distribution strategy was also unconventional, with Swatch watches sold exclusively in high-end department stores and reputable watch shops, as well as in mini-boutiques and fashion-accessory

stores. Despite having a limited number of designs, the Swatch team ensured that each design was strategically placed in relevant outlets, such
as watersports-themed watches being sold near lakes and snow sport–
themed watches in mountainous regions.

Swatch's pricing strategy further reinforced its positioning as a fashion
accessory. The watches were priced lower than other Swiss-made watches
and maintained consistent pricing across all models, making them affordable and perfect for impulse purchases. The communication strategy was
equally unconventional, with bold and creative advertising that deviated
from the norms of the watch industry.

Central to Swatch's success was also its ability to integrate Swiss cultural narratives into its branding. The "Swiss-made" label, synonymous
with precision, tradition, and craftsmanship, was prominently featured
on every Swatch. This cultural association played a crucial role in differentiating Swatch from its competitors, positioning even a playful, affordable
product as a symbol of Swiss quality.

This narrative extended beyond Swatch to the Group's higher-end
brands, such as Omega and Tissot. By emphasizing Swiss heritage and
blending it with modern design, these brands resonated with a global
audience seeking both authenticity and innovation. This strategic use of
cultural identity not only bolstered consumer trust but also allowed the
Swatch Group to redefine luxury for a broader audience, turning it into
"affordable luxury" while retaining an aspirational appeal.

None of the marketing mix elements used by Swatch were typical of either the jewelry subcategory (e.g., luxurious Swiss timepieces
or affordable Japanese watches mimicking Swiss designs) or the tool
watch subcategory (like Timex). Instead, Swatch borrowed from the
fashion-accessory category and applied these elements consistently and
with meticulous attention to detail, transforming consumer perception
of the product.

While jewelry is often seen as serious and timeless, fashion accessories are typically playful and seasonally relevant. Jewelry purchases tend
to be deliberate and considered, whereas fashion accessories are more
commonly driven by impulse. By applying a consistent and unconventional approach across its entire marketing mix, Swatch successfully repositioned its watches as fashion accessories, encouraging spontaneous

purchases, multiple ownership, and a shift from rational to emotional buying behavior.

This product positioning strategy also led to a shift in consumer purchasing criteria, from focusing on timekeeping accuracy and craftsmanship to prioritizing emotional appeal and subjective value. As a result, Swatch attracted a younger market segment that had previously shown little interest in watches. The success of Swatch ultimately contributed to the growth and diversification of the overall watch market, with the fashion-accessory subcategory now including major players like Timex and Fossil, as well as numerous fashion brands ranging from premium labels like Armani to high-street brands like Zara.

In summary, a successful breakaway strategy hinges on the ability to borrow and adapt associations from unrelated product categories, using the entire marketing mix with precision and consistency to create a distinctive brand perception. This strategy often requires the development of new internal capabilities, as Swatch did by pioneering manufacturing innovations, forging novel retail partnerships, and communicating in unconventional ways. A comprehensive, consistent, and almost obsessive marketing strategy is essential to effectively communicate the product's reinvention to consumers, with meticulous attention to detail and unwavering consistency across all touchpoints to ensure the message resonates cohesively.

Sources and Further Readings

Govindarajan, V., and C. Trimble. 2010. *The Other Side of Innovation: Solving the Execution Challenge.* Harvard Business Press.

Hutter, K., and S. Hoffmann. 2011. "Guerrilla Marketing: The Nature of the Concept and Propositions for Further Research." *Asian Journal of Marketing* 5: 39–54.

Kelley, T., and D. Kelley. 2013. *Creative Confidence: Unleashing the Creative Potential Within Us All.* Crown Business.

Kotler, P., K. L. Keller, and A. Chernev. 2021. *Marketing Management, Global Edition.* Pearson.

Leung, F. F., F. F. Gu, Y. Li, J. Z. Zhang, and R. W. Palmatier. 2022. "Influencer Marketing Effectiveness." *Journal of Marketing* 86 (6): 93–115.

Levinson, J. C. 2007. *Guerrilla Marketing: Easy and Inexpensive Strategies for Making Big Profits from Your Small Business.* 4th ed. Houghton Mifflin Harcourt.

Moon, Y. 2005. *Break Free from the Product Life Cycle.* Harvard Business Review Press.

Moon, Y. 2010. *Different: Escaping the Competitive Herd.* Harvard Business Review Press.

Radjou, N., J. Prabhu, and S. Ahuja. 2012. *Jugaad Innovation: Think Frugal, Be Flexible, Generate Breakthrough Growth.* Wiley.

Schmitt, B. 2011. *Experiential Marketing: How to Get Customers to Feel, Think, and Act.* Free Press.

Scott, D. M. 2024. *The New Rules of Marketing and PR.* Wiley.

Sharp, B. 2010. *How Brands Grow: What Marketers Don't Know.* Oxford University Press.

CHAPTER 8

The Outcome and Closing Reflections

In March 1983, the Swatch marketing team faced a daunting challenge. They had no clear idea of how many watches they could sell in each market, and their budget was too tight for extensive market research. To make matters worse, they were surrounded by naysayers who constantly voiced doubts and negativity about the project.

The limited market research they managed to conduct was disheartening, offering little hope. At that point, the Swatch launch could have easily seemed like a lost cause. However, in the weeks leading up to the Zurich press conference, Theile took a different approach. He reflected on the upcoming launch and began meticulously creating a list of target countries, carefully assigning a sales target to each one. Gradually, he added up the 1 million watches that Thomke had promised could be produced in 1983, writing by hand his targets on a piece of paper: 30,000 watches in Switzerland, 60,000 in the UK, 150,000 between Germany and France, and so on.

The list wasn't the product of complex data analysis or detailed forecasts; it was driven by the company's capabilities, manufacturing capacity, and, most importantly, intuition. Unsurprisingly, Theile's projections turned out to be far from accurate—not because they fell short, but because they were wildly exceeded. Sales targets for each market were not just met; they were surpassed at an astonishing pace (Figure 8.1).

Within weeks, Swatch watches were flying off the shelves, stunning everyone involved. The company sold far more watches than initially budgeted for, particularly in Switzerland, where the public embraced the Swatch brand and its mission to save the Swiss watch industry. In the first few months alone, an incredible 350,000 Swatches were sold in Switzerland, smashing the original target of 30,000.

	Sales target	Units sold
Switzerland	30,000	350,000
UK	60,000	140,000
Germany	80,000	140,000
France	70,000	120,000
United States	100,000	250,000
Italy	50,000	0
Spain	40,000	0
BeNeLux	50,000	0
Scandinavia	50,000	0
Austria	20,000	0
TOTAL		1,000,000

*Figure 8.1 Swatch sales targets vs. actual units sold in 1983.
Markets with no sales experienced stock depletion due to unexpectedly
high demand, delaying entry*

This overwhelming success, however, introduced new challenges. Swatch simply could not produce enough watches to satisfy the soaring demand across all markets simultaneously. Consequently, the launches in Germany and France had to be postponed by several months, while those in Italy and Spain were pushed back until 1984.

Theile found himself grappling with mixed emotions after selling their first million watches. On one hand, the achievement was a source of immense joy, but, on the other, it highlighted a significant problem: Swatch's production capacity could not keep pace with demand. By the end of the first year, Swatch was only able to produce 10,000 watches per day, necessitating a rapid expansion to meet the surging sales figures.

Despite the production bottlenecks and the uncertainty that surrounded its launch, Swatch ultimately rose to the occasion. The team found ways to scale up operations, stabilize supply, and coordinate international rollouts effectively. What initially seemed like insurmountable obstacles became powerful catalysts for learning, innovation, and agility. Within just a few years, Swatch was not only meeting global demand; it was reshaping the whole industry.

This book has argued that the Swatch saga offers a wealth of lessons and insights, not only for watch enthusiasts but also for anyone interested in business and marketing. It illuminates the power of innovation, branding, strategic market management, and cultural resonance.

Although Swatch's success was not solely the result of meticulous planning, its journey was interwoven with critical elements that fuelled its remarkable ascent. From the disruptive power of innovation and collaboration to the boldness of pushing boundaries with a mix of naivety and audacious flair, Swatch embodied a spirit of ingenuity and adaptability that redefined traditional strategic planning.

The Swatch tale challenges the conventional wisdom that success must be painstakingly engineered, instead offering a testament to the profound impact of spontaneity, creativity, and resilience. Yet, while many factors contributing to Swatch's success may not have been the result of careful, systematic planning, our innate curiosity compels us to extract valuable lessons. These insights, whether replicable or simply instructive in hindsight, offer a roadmap for navigating the unpredictable terrain of business innovation and success.

The success of Swatch and its team's ability to adapt and improvise can be analyzed through many lenses. As noted, one of them is arguably Mintzberg's concept of emergent strategy, which emphasizes the importance of flexibility, adaptability, and learning through action.

Swatch's success was not solely the product of a meticulously crafted master plan; it was, to a large extent, the result of adaptive responses to evolving circumstances and shifting market dynamics. The Swatch marketing team exhibited a sharp awareness of emerging trends and consumer preferences, enabling them to act swiftly and seize opportunities as they arose. By consistently experimenting with various tactics, watch designs, and elements of the marketing mix, they were able to iterate and refine their strategy in real-time, tailoring their approach to each market segment. This agile mindset allowed them to leverage market feedback effectively, using it to inform and guide their subsequent decisions.

A Tale of Market-Driving Strategy

The Swatch launch is fundamentally also a story about successful radical innovation in a mature market. Its launch stands out as a prime example of a market-driving strategy, distinct from a market-driven approach.

Market-driven strategies typically involve understanding and responding to existing customer preferences within a given market structure. Companies following this approach focus on incremental innovation, tending to rely a lot on customer input to drive product development. While this approach is often a very effective way for an organization to be customer-centric and generate incremental innovations that create value for both customers and brands, it can overlook new trends and opportunities.

In contrast, market-driving strategies involve actively shaping things like the market structure and the behavior of players within that market (e.g., customers) to enhance the competitive position of the business. Companies pursuing this strategy aim to create new market spaces and drive radical innovation that can change the market structure, customer behavior, or both. This approach is riskier but offers the potential for significant rewards and market leadership.

Classic examples of market-driving innovations include the Apple iPod, IKEA, Netflix, Amazon, Airbnb, Benetton, Uber, and Gatorade. All these brands can be considered radical innovations that have disrupted industries to create new demand. They identified incipient needs (i.e., needs that customers were not fully aware of) and developed innovative solutions to address them.

Airbnb, for example, revolutionized the hospitality industry by offering travelers a unique accommodation experience that most people did not realize they needed until it was presented to them. It would have been unimaginable before Airbnb's market entry that the leading supplier of lodging in the world would not own any lodging of its own.

Similarly, prior to the arrival of the Swatch, it was unlikely that anyone would have considered the necessity of a low-cost, vibrant, Swiss-made timepiece fashioned from plastic. By challenging existing market norms and changing customer perceptions, market-driven propositions can carve out unique competitive advantages and achieve remarkable success. Swatch is a perfect example.

The Swatch launch exemplifies a market-driving strategy for several compelling reasons. First and foremost, Swatch didn't simply enter the existing watch market—it created an entirely new segment. Rather than focusing solely on functionality, Swatch positioned its watches as fashion accessories, appealing to a much broader audience beyond traditional watch buyers. Swatch successfully targeted a previously overlooked younger demographic, while also attracting mature consumers seeking stylish watches at an affordable price. By doing so, Swatch carved out a unique market segment for budget-friendly yet fashionable watches, sidestepping direct competition with established brands and establishing its own niche.

Swatch's broad market appeal, catering to a diverse range of consumers from fashion-forward youth to budget-conscious adults, was pivotal to its success. The brand didn't just capture existing watch buyers; it also enticed people who had never owned a watch to make a purchase—sometimes even multiple purchases—thereby expanding the overall market.

Another hallmark of Swatch as a market-driving concept was its foundation in radical innovation, which reshaped customer perceptions and behaviors. The integration of modular construction, quartz technology, plastic casing, injection molding, and ultrasonic welding in watchmaking was groundbreaking at the time, setting Swatch apart from its competitors.

Strategically, Swatch used clever marketing and branding to establish a breakaway positioning strategy and position itself as a symbol of individuality, creativity, and lifestyle. By tapping into the cultural zeitgeist and aligning with emerging trends, Swatch cultivated a distinct brand identity that resonated with consumers globally. This ability to shape both the market and consumer behavior solidified Swatch's role as a true market driver.

The disruptive distribution model also challenged the conventional retail channels dominated by luxury watch brands, such as jewelers. The use of standalone retail outlets with high footfall, like airports and shopping malls, was completely unorthodox. This direct-to-consumer approach allowed Swatch to control its brand image, enhance customer experience, and reach a broader audience.

Ultimately, the optimal strategic approach for a company hinges on its goals, resources, and risk tolerance. While market-driven strategies provide stability and incremental growth by capitalizing on existing opportunities, market-driving strategies hold the potential for transformative change and long-term competitiveness. Many organizations adopt a balanced approach, investing in market-driven activities to sustain current success while also pursuing market-driving initiatives to fuel future growth and innovation.

In the case of Swatch, a market-driving strategy was particularly well-suited due to the innovative nature of its product, its distinct market positioning, and the company's willingness to embrace risk. Swatch didn't merely respond to existing consumer demands; it reshaped consumer behavior in a mature industry by creating an entirely new market segment.

Moreover, Swatch had relatively little to lose by adopting a market-driving strategy. The watch industry was in decline, and only a radical, risk-laden move could have altered its trajectory. This context provided Swatch with the freedom—and perhaps the necessity—to take risks and pursue bold, unconventional strategies. This, of course, is not to diminish the creativity and courage of their pioneering team, whose vision and audacity were crucial in redefining an industry and ensuring the brand's enduring success.

If Swatch were to launch today, leveraging blitzscaling—a strategy focused on rapid, aggressive growth—could significantly amplify its impact. Coined by LinkedIn cofounder Reid Hoffman, *blitzscaling* draws inspiration from the military tactic "blitzkrieg," which emphasized speed and surprise to overwhelm opponents before they could defend themselves.

In business, blitzscaling prioritizes rapid expansion over efficiency, with the aim of quickly achieving market dominance. The core principle is that, in certain industries—especially tech—speed can be more valuable than efficiency, as being the first mover often leads to market control. For a brand like Swatch, blitzscaling could enable rapid global expansion, allowing it to capitalize on its disruptive innovation and capture new consumer segments before competitors can respond. It could facilitate rapid market entry, accelerated product line growth, engagement with digital communities, building global brand awareness, and efficiently scaling its supply chain. By executing on these fronts, a brand like Swatch today could turn its bold market-driving strategy into an unprecedented growth success.

At the heart of blitzscaling is the trade-off between speed and risk, where companies accept operational inefficiencies, resource overextension, and high burn rates in exchange for fast growth. Companies like

Facebook, Airbnb, and Uber exemplify how blitzscaling can lead to market dominance. They embraced bold risks, rapidly expanded operations, and accepted potential instability for the chance at market leadership.

Blue Ocean Strategy

The concept of market-driving strategy shares notable similarities with the blue ocean strategy, as briefly mentioned in Chapter 6. This framework offers a valuable lens through which to analyze Swatch's success.

Blue ocean strategy posits that businesses can achieve significant success by creating uncontested market spaces, or "blue oceans," rather than competing in overcrowded, saturated markets, known as "red oceans." The introduction of the Swatch watch is a textbook example of a blue ocean strategy in action. At the time when the traditional watch industry was dominated by high-priced luxury mechanical watches targeting an older, affluent demographic, the primary alternative consisted of inexpensive Japanese quartz watches. Swatch disrupted this landscape by appealing to a younger, fashion-conscious audience with stylish, high-quality yet affordable, mass-produced quartz watches. This strategic shift created a new market space distinct from the existing watch industry, effectively bypassing direct competition with established players.

A central concept in blue ocean strategy is the *value curve*, also known as the *strategy canvas*. This graphical tool illustrates a company's competitive position within its industry across key factors of competition. The value curve plots a company's offerings against those of its competitors along various attributes important to customers, such as price, quality, features, and customer service. Each attribute is represented on the horizontal axis, while the vertical axis indicates the level of offering for each attribute, reflecting the extent to which a company invests in and emphasizes specific competitive factors.

The canvas itself demonstrates how a company's offering compares to those of its competitors across these attributes. A higher curve for a particular attribute indicates that the company's offering is perceived as superior to its competitors in that area. This allows companies to visualize their competitive position relative to rivals and identify areas where they excel, meet basic expectations, or underperform. It also helps them understand the broader industry landscape, assess customer value, and uncover new strategic opportunities.

By using the strategy canvas, companies can develop strategies to differentiate themselves from competitors and create a unique value proposition. This could involve reallocating resources to enhance areas where they are lagging, reducing emphasis on factors overemphasized by competitors, or introducing entirely new competitive factors that redefine industry standards. Ultimately, the goal of the strategy canvas is to guide companies toward uncontested market spaces, where they can create new value for customers and unlock opportunities for growth and innovation.

A classic example of the strategy canvas in action is the Australian winemaker Yellow Tail and its entry into the U.S. wine market. Before Yellow Tail's arrival, the market was polarized, with premium and budget winemakers dominating the landscape. The traditional factors of competition included a wine's aging quality, vineyard prestige, complexity, the use of oenological terminology, and, of course, price. Premium winemakers excelled in these areas, while budget brands competed on the same metrics but with lower investments. Yellow Tail disrupted this entrenched landscape by fundamentally altering its value curve in three key ways compared to existing players.

First, Yellow Tail raised factors related to accessibility and simplicity, making wine more appealing to a broader audience. Second, it reduced emphasis on vineyard prestige, aging quality, wine range, and complexity, while eliminating confusing oenological terminology from labels—often perceived as pretentious—thus removing the need for extensive wine knowledge or experience. Third, Yellow Tail created a new market space by introducing entirely new competitive factors, such as easy-drinking flavors, ease of selection, and a sense of fun and adventure in a wine brand—elements previously absent from the wine industry. This combination of raising, reducing, eliminating, and creating factors of competition made Yellow Tail approachable, particularly to non-wine drinkers (a highly profitable blue ocean), leading to its phenomenal success.

Similarly, Swatch redefined industry standards to craft a new value proposition and value curve with its marketing mix. Swatch reduced or eliminated factors such as complexity, unnecessary features, high prices, the use of precious materials, and traditional craftsmanship. Instead, the brand offered simple, colorful designs at a fraction of the cost of traditional watches. By focusing on functionality and fashion while reducing costs, Swatch delivered significant value to customers. At the same time, Swatch raised factors like accessibility, offering a wide range of fashionable designs and making watches more appealing to a younger audience.

Crucially, Swatch also created new competitive factors by introducing fashion-forward designs that invited self-expression into the watch industry, establishing an avant-garde brand that resonated with the lifestyle aspirations of its target market. The launch of Swatch exemplifies a blue ocean strategy by successfully creating a new market space, redefining industry boundaries, and delivering unmatched value to customers through a unique value curve. By raising, reducing, eliminating, and creating factors of competition, Swatch carved out its own uncontested market niche, positioning itself for unprecedented success in the global watch industry.

A strong strategy curve that represents a sustainable competitive advantage typically exhibits three key characteristics. First, it demonstrates focus by strategically narrowing down the dimensions on which the company competes, emphasizing certain aspects while consciously deciding to forgo others. This ensures clarity and coherence in the value proposition, making it easier for the company to excel in its chosen areas. Second, it showcases divergence by boldly breaking away from industry conventions and norms, challenging the status quo with novel approaches and offerings that capture customer attention. This distinctiveness sets the company apart from its competitors, creating a unique market position. Third, it lends itself to the creation of a compelling tagline—a succinct and memorable phrase that effectively communicates the essence of the curve's unique value proposition. This helps differentiate the company and leaves a lasting impression on customers.

Swatch's strategy canvas exemplifies these principles. Its focus on design, fashion, affordability, and high quality sharply diverged from traditional industry norms. And by pioneering the iconic tagline "Fashion accessory that tells time," Swatch encapsulated its innovative approach in a nutshell, effectively communicating its unique value proposition to the market (Figure 8.2).

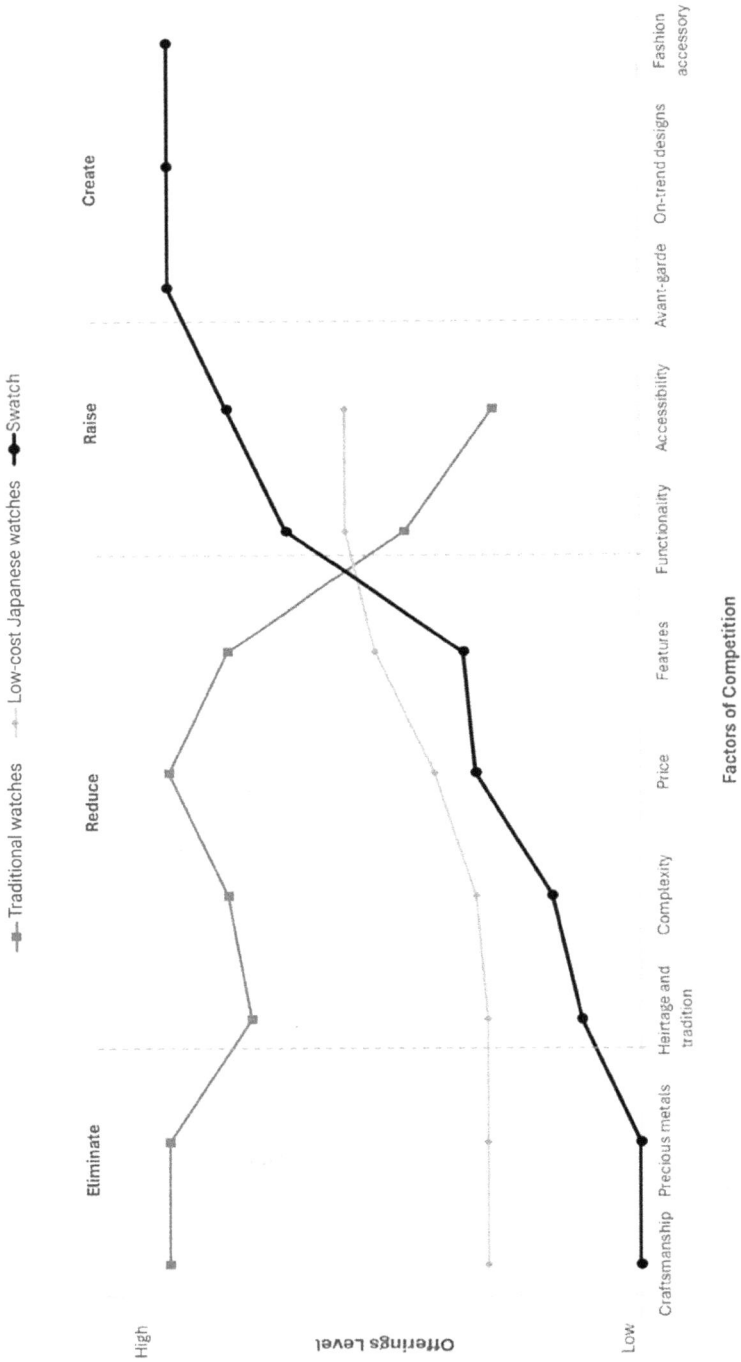

Figure 8.2 Depiction of a potential strategy canvas illustrating Swatch's differentiation upon entering the market in the 1980s

Other Theoretical Lenses

With the benefit of hindsight, Swatch's success can appear almost inevitable; something that slots neatly into various established theories in strategy, marketing, and organizational behavior. And indeed, powerful additional conceptual lenses (such as the Resource-Based View of the firm, disruptive innovation, or change management, just to name a few) can also offer compelling explanations for how Swatch turned crisis into competitive advantage. But we must be careful not to confuse clarity in retrospect with foresight in the moment. Theory is tidy; execution is messy. For the managers, engineers, and marketers behind Swatch, success was far from preordained. Their task was not to explain a triumph but to make it happen, in real-time, amid industry collapse, internal resistance, and high uncertainty. These theoretical perspectives, then, are not presented here to romanticize the past or over-intellectualize the story. Rather, they help us reflect on the mechanisms that, in hindsight, might have contributed to Swatch's breakthrough, and which may serve today as additional tools and references that decision-makers might want to use to shape their own futures.

For example, the Resource-Based View (RBV) of the firm, a strategic management theory popularized by Jay Barney, can provide a valuable perspective on Swatch's competitive advantage. The RBV emphasizes that a firm's resources and capabilities are critical to achieving and sustaining a competitive edge. Swatch's resources included its deep expertise in Swiss watchmaking, its innovative use of materials like plastic, and the strong brand equity associated with the "Swiss-made" tagline. However, it was Swatch's capabilities, such as its ability to innovate quickly, its ability to understand market trends, its efficient production processes, and its distinctive marketing approach to emotionalize the product, that truly set it apart from competitors. By leveraging these unique resources and capabilities, Swatch was able to create a product that was not only distinctive but also difficult for competitors to replicate, thereby securing a lasting competitive advantage.

Dynamic capabilities theory (pioneered by Teece, Pisano, and Shuen) is built on the RBV, but it emphasizes a company's ability to integrate, build, and reconfigure internal and external competencies to address rapidly changing environments. It focuses on the processes through which firms can sustain a competitive advantage in dynamic markets. Swatch's success could also be analyzed through this lens. As the Swiss watch industry faced the quartz crisis, Swatch's leadership demonstrated a keen ability to sense opportunities in the mass market for affordable, fashionable watches. They quickly seized this opportunity by restructuring production processes, employing plastic materials, and simplifying the assembly line. Swatch's ability to integrate cutting-edge technology with new consumer demands highlights how effectively deploying dynamic capabilities can turn industry threats into business advantages.

Michael Porter's Five Forces Framework offers an additional lens through which one could analyze Swatch's competitive positioning within the watch industry. The framework identifies five key forces: the threat of new entrants, the bargaining power of suppliers, the bargaining power of buyers, the threat of substitutes, and the intensity of competitive rivalry. Swatch mitigated the threat of new entrants by establishing strong brand recognition, customer loyalty, and economies of scale. It reduced supplier power through vertical integration and maintained buyer power by offering a unique combination of affordability and style as well as constant new designs. Swatch also managed the threat of substitutes by differentiating its products through innovative design, and it lessened competitive rivalry by creating a new market segment with its Swiss-made, fashionable, affordable watches.

Clayton Christensen's Disruptive Innovation Theory also provides a compelling lens through which one could examine Swatch's success. The theory explains how simpler, more affordable products can disrupt established markets by initially targeting niche segments and eventually moving upmarket, displacing established competitors. Swatch exemplified disruptive innovation by introducing a product that, while simpler and cheaper, redefined consumer expectations. It began by appealing to a demographic that traditional Swiss watches had overlooked, namely, young consumers and those seeking affordability without compromising on style. Over time, Swatch's strong brand appeal and continuous innovation allowed it to capture a larger market share, disrupting both the higher-end watch segment and the mass-market quartz segment.

John Kotter's Eight-Step Change Model could offer another perspective, particularly in analyzing how Swatch successfully navigated the organizational changes required to launch and establish the brand. Kotter's model outlines eight critical steps for effective change management, including creating a sense of urgency, forming a powerful coalition, and generating short-term wins. One could argue that Swatch's leadership created a sense of urgency by recognizing the existential threat posed by the quartz crisis to the Swiss watch industry. An effective team of engineers, designers, and marketers was formed to drive the Swatch project forward. The early success of Swatch, evidenced by its rapid market adoption, initial consumer wins, and strong sales, served as short-term wins that fuelled further momentum and organizational commitment to the brand's long-term success.

Swatch's success could also be examined through Edgar Schein's Organizational Culture Model, which highlights the profound impact of organizational culture on a company's performance. Schein's model focuses on three levels of culture: artifacts, espoused values, and basic underlying assumptions. Thomke was instrumental in shaping a culture that fostered innovation, agility, and a willingness to challenge industry norms. The visible artifacts, such as the playful and colorful designs of the watches, reflected the company's creative ethos. The espoused values emphasized affordability, style, and quality, which were consistently communicated both internally and externally. At the deepest level, Swatch's basic assumptions revolved around the belief that a watch could be more than just a timekeeping device. It could be an affordable, fashionable accessory accessible to all. This strong cultural alignment across all levels was a key factor in Swatch's ability to innovate and successfully disrupt the market.

The S-Curve theory of innovation could also help explain Swatch's rise, as the brand successfully navigated the phases of innovation adoption by embracing quartz technology early, while traditional Swiss watchmakers lagged. Using Everett M. Rogers' Diffusion of Innovations theory, Swatch's success can be attributed to its ability to appeal to early adopters through bold, fashionable designs that resonated with trendsetters and younger consumers. These early adopters helped Swatch build momentum, allowing it to cross the "chasm" and reach the mainstream market. Key factors that contributed to Swatch's widespread adoption include its relative advantage (offering a stylish, affordable, and reliable alternative to traditional watches) and its compatibility with consumer preferences for fashion and personal expression. Additionally, Swatch's simplicity made it accessible, and its communicability was amplified through vibrant marketing and striking product designs. The brand's affordability also encouraged trialability, allowing consumers to experiment with different designs easily. These factors combined to help Swatch move from niche appeal to mainstream dominance.

Finally, one could also argue that Swatch's product development process was deeply rooted in design thinking (even if the term itself wasn't explicitly used at the time), which focuses on human-centered innovation. The brand identified that watches could be no longer just functional devices but also fashion statements. This shift in perspective allowed Swatch to redefine the market by designing a product that prioritized aesthetics, simplicity, and affordability. Swatch's use of bold colors, interchangeable bands, and accessible pricing demonstrated a keen understanding of customer desires, blending functionality with emotional appeal. Through iterative prototyping, Swatch continually refined its designs, ensuring that each product resonated with the needs and preferences of its diverse audience.

The theories discussed here represent only a selection of the many frameworks that one could apply to analyze Swatch's success with the benefit of hindsight. The management, marketing, strategy, and entrepreneurship toolkits are replete with concepts and theories that, when applied retrospectively, can help explain a brand's meteoric rise. But the real challenge, of course, is not to find theories that fit a story already written; it is to use these tools before the outcome is known. For business leaders, the real test is applying insight in the face of ambiguity, resistance, and risk. Hindsight offers 20/20 vision, but Swatch's success was achieved without that clarity, built instead in the fog of uncertainty, by people who dared to act boldly, move quickly, and challenge convention (in part because they had little choice). That, perhaps more than anything else, is the enduring lesson of the Swatch story.

Looking Back to Look Forward

In summary, the Swatch launch, viewed through a marketing lens, exemplifies powerful concepts such as market-driving strategy, blue ocean strategy, and breakaway positioning. Rather than following existing demand, Swatch redefined it, creating new market space, reshaping consumer expectations, and sparking desire where none previously existed. In doing so, it tapped into incipient customer needs: unspoken wants that consumers themselves hadn't yet identified. This leads to an enduring challenge for innovators and marketers alike: How can companies uncover such hidden needs before they become obvious? If customers can't articulate what they want, traditional tools like surveys and focus groups may prove insufficient. Anticipating demand, rather than reacting to it, requires a different mindset, one that values empathy, imagination, and the courage to act without certainty.

A quote often (though dubiously) attributed to Henry Ford captures this spirit: "If I had asked my customers what they wanted, they would have said a faster horse." Regardless of its origin, the sentiment reflects a deeper truth about innovation. Ford didn't simply improve the known. He redefined what was possible by understanding underlying human desires. Swatch did the same. It recognized that watches could be more than instruments for telling time; they could be fashion accessories, cultural symbols, and expressions of individuality. In this way, Swatch didn't just enter a market; it reinvented one.

The launch of Swatch marked a turning point for the struggling Swiss watch industry. Through a blend of product innovation, process optimization, and creative marketing, it generated commercial success while significantly improving the financial performance of ETA. The brand's market entry pressured dominant Japanese quartz watchmakers to reconsider their pricing strategies. By offering affordable, Swiss-made watches at scale, Swatch set a new value benchmark, stabilizing the industry and reaffirming Switzerland's global watchmaking relevance.

But Swatch's impact extended well beyond its own brand. It lifted the profile of other Swiss marques like Rado, Longines, Tissot, and Omega, demonstrating the power of interdependence in the industry's ecosystem. Even the heritage-driven, craftsmanship-focused segments benefited from the renewed global prestige of the "Swiss-made" label. By the end of the decade, Swiss exports had rebounded, and the country had regained market share across both high-price and low-price segments, showing that innovation and tradition could not only coexist but thrive together.

Of course, this turnaround was driven by more than branding and bold ideas. Structural reform, especially the rationalization of production, played a vital role. Centralizing and integrating manufacturing helped eliminate inefficiencies, cut costs, and unlock economies of scale, critical in competing with low-cost international players. At the same time, the industry reasserted its Swiss identity, embedding quality, elegance, and technical mastery in the "Swiss-made" promise, values Swatch cleverly reimagined for a younger, broader audience.

A key milestone in this transformation was the consolidation of ASUAG and SSIH into the Swatch Group. This merger brought together luxury and mass-market brands under a cohesive strategic vision. By centralizing decision making while preserving brand distinctiveness, the Swatch Group scaled effectively, increased market share, and reduced overdependence on any single brand or segment. The result was not only long-term profitability but also stability across the portfolio.

Swatch's mastery of both economies of scale and scope played a central role in its rise. By producing high volumes, it distributed fixed costs efficiently, allowing for competitive pricing without sacrificing margins. Meanwhile, its constant stream of design iterations catered to diverse tastes while maintaining operational efficiency, an exemplary model of scalable personalization. This agility helped Swatch remain relevant across generations and global markets.

Under Nicolas Hayek's leadership, the Swatch Group embraced vertical integration, bold marketing, and talent retention, fuelling growth across both the Swatch brand and its premium counterparts. The Swatch Group's strategic balance between affordability and aspiration generated a powerful halo effect: making the whole greater than the sum of its parts. The emotional resonance of Swatch helped anchor the group, while its profitability supported the revival of high-end mechanical watchmaking.

Over four decades, Swatch has demonstrated a rare resilience, rooted in what might be called "brand immunity," a combination of emotional engagement, brand commitment, and a robust ecosystem. It has withstood industry disruption, shifting trends, and evolving consumer expectations through a careful mix of strategic discipline and creative risk-taking. Its next test lies in navigating the rise of smartwatches and digital wearables, where relevance will depend on Swatch's continued ability to blend heritage with innovation.

Perhaps the most symbolic testament to Swatch's legacy is that it became the namesake of the entire group, outshining even prestigious brands like Omega and Tissot. That one bold, colorful, and affordable plastic watch could revitalize an entire industry is more than a business case; it's a reminder of what's possible when creativity, ingenuity, and purpose converge. The Swatch story isn't just about saving an industry; it's about reimagining what an industry could be. It's a testament to the power of vision, design, and timing (mixed with just enough audacity and good fortune). In the end, Swatch left more than a mark on its own industry; it offered lessons that could help reshape any industry.

Sources and Further Readings

Barney, J. B. 1991. "Firm Resources and Sustained Competitive Advantage." *Journal of Management* 17 (1): 99–120.

Brown, T. 2009. *Change by Design: How Design Thinking Transforms Organisations and Inspires Innovation.* Harper Collins.

Christensen, C. M. 1997. *The Innovator's Dilemma: When New Technologies Cause Great Firms to Fail.* Harvard Business School Press.

Christensen, C. M., M. E. Raynor, and R. McDonald. 2015. "What Is Disruptive Innovation?" *Harvard Business Review* 93 (12): 44–53.

Cross, N. 2011. *Design Thinking: Understanding How Designers Think and Work.* Bloomsbury Academic.

Hoffman, R., and C. Yeh. 2018. *Blitzscaling: The Lightning-Fast Path to Building Massively Valuable Companies.* Currency.

Jaworski, B. J., A. K. Kohli, and A. Sahay. 2000. "Market-Driven Versus Driving Markets." *Journal of the Academy of Marketing Science* 28 (1): 45–53.

Kim, W. C., and R. Mauborgne. 2005. "Blue Ocean Strategy: From Theory to Practice—Strategy Canvas." *Harvard Business Review* 83 (10): 58–67.

Kim, W. C., and R. Mauborgne. 2015. *Blue Ocean Strategy: How to Create Uncontested Market Space and Make the Competition Irrelevant.* 10th Anniversary ed. Harvard Business Review Press.

Kotter, J. P. 1996. *Leading Change.* Harvard Business Review Press.

Lewin, K. 1947. "Frontiers in Group Dynamics: Concept, Method and Reality in Social Science. Social Equilibrium and Social Change." *Human Relations* 1 (1): 5–41.

Liedtka, J., and T. Ogilvie. 2011. *Designing for Growth: A Design Thinking Tool Kit for Managers*. Columbia University Press.

Mauborgne, R., and W. C. Kim. 2010. "Blue Ocean Strategy: How to Break Out of the Red Ocean and Create New Market Space." *Strategic Management Journal* 31 (2): 123–142.

Merlo, O., A. B. Eisingerich, and W. D. Hoyer. 2024. "Immunizing Customers Against Negative Brand-Related Information." *Journal of the Academy of Marketing Science* 52 (1): 140–163.

Porter, M. E. 1980. *Competitive Strategy: Techniques for Analyzing Industries and Competitors*. Free Press.

Rogers, E. M. 2003. *Diffusion of Innovations*. 5th ed. Free Press.

Schein, E. H. 2010. *Organizational Culture and Leadership*. 4th ed. Jossey-Bass.

Senge, P. M. 1990. *The Fifth Discipline: The Art & Practice of the Learning Organization*. Doubleday.

Teece, D. J., G. Pisano, and A. Shuen. 1997. "Dynamic Capabilities and Strategic Management." *Strategic Management Journal* 18 (7): 509–533.

Verganti, R. 2009. *Design-Driven Innovation: Changing the Rules of Competition by Radically Innovating What Things Mean*. Harvard Business Review Press.

About the Authors

Dr. Omar Merlo is Associate Professor of Marketing Strategy and Academic Director at Imperial Business School. He was previously a lecturer at Cambridge University and the University of Melbourne, where he also earned his PhD. He has held visiting appointments at institutions including Oxford, LSE, UCL, ETH Zurich, EPFL, Lausanne, Lugano, and Aalto University. His research on marketing strategy, services, and branding has appeared in journals such as *Journal of Marketing, JAMS, Journal of Service Research*, and *MIT Sloan Management Review*. As an adviser, he has worked with many global firms, including McKinsey, Airbus, Unilever, Samsung, Audi, Nissan, Petronas, ABB, Barclays, and HSBC.

Dr. Konstantin Theile is a guest lecturer at Imperial Business School and several other universities. He was formerly Professor of International Marketing, Business Ethics and Entrepreneurship at ESB Business School, Reutlingen University, and Director at the Swiss Research Institute of Small Business and Entrepreneurship at the University of St. Gallen. After earning his doctorate in economics from St. Gallen, he worked at UBS and Hoffmann-La Roche. In 1982, he joined the watch industry to establish and lead the global marketing strategy for Swatch. He later founded several companies and now works as a business adviser.

Index

www.ingramcontent.com/pod-product-compliance
Lightning Source LLC
Chambersburg PA
CBHW061306220326
41599CB00026B/4760